Feeling Good

FEELING GOOD

Hugh Buckingham

EPWORTH PRESS

British Library Cataloguing in Publication Data
Buckingham, Hugh
    Feeling good.
    1. Life.   Philosophical perspectives
    I. Title
    128'.5

ISBN 0–7162–0460–6

First published 1989 by
Epworth Press
Room 195, 1 Central Buildings, Westminster
London SW1H 9NR

Phototypeset by J&L Composition Ltd,
Filey, North Yorkshire
and printed in Great Britain by
Richard Clay Ltd, Bungay, Suffolk

Contents

1

The Chaos of our Emotions

One of the books that I used to enjoy reading to my children when they were young is called *The Little Brute Family*.[1] A picture book and very short, it was about a family of odd-looking and sour creatures who lived dismally in the middle of a dark wood.

In the morning Mama cooked a sand and gravel porridge, and the family snarled and grimaced as they spooned it up. No one said, 'Please'. No one said, 'Thank you', and no one said, 'How delicious', because it was not delicious. Baby Brute howled between spoonfuls. Brother and sister kicked each other under the table.

The expected transformation of this depressing scene came about in the following way.

One day Baby Brute found a little wandering lost good feeling in a field of daisies, and he caught it in his paw and put it in his tiny pocket. And he felt so good that he laughed and said, 'How lovely'. Baby Brute felt good all afternoon, and at supper when his bowl was filled with stew he said, 'Thank you'. Then the little good feeling flew out of his tiny pocket and hovered over the table, humming and smiling.

Satisfactorily the little good feeling decided to stay with the family and 'when springtime came again the little Brute family changed their name to "Nice"'.

What struck me about this simple story, when I first began

thinking seriously about our feelings and emotions, was the way it drew attention to the apparent helplessness of the Brute family in their misery and to the complete independence of 'the little good feeling'. The family were wholly at the mercy of events. They were not responsible for their unhappiness or their vindictive behaviour. They felt bad. That was how they were. It was just luck that Baby Brute happened to come upon 'the little good feeling'. The feeling did not seem to belong anywhere or to anyone. It wasn't clear where it came from. There was no indication of how or why it took root first in the Baby and then in the whole Brute family nor of whether it was likely to remain once it had arrived.

The story contains the sort of mysteries that often confront us when we first start looking at our emotions and feelings. We don't understand them. Although they are so much a part of us and have the power to make us wildly excited or to fling us into despair, we can't quite grasp hold of them. They are like mercury, changing shape too fast, moving in odd directions, slipping through our fingers or unexpectedly coagulating. It's been like that since we can first remember.

We know roughly the sort of way we have often felt in different circumstances and these root feelings of ours must, we assume, have been caused in some way but the process does not seem amenable to rational analysis. Perhaps we have been none too anxious to explore very far for fear that we may become open to more guilt than we already bear.

People might tell us for example, 'You have a calm temperament', and it is true that we are not usually ruffled and people like to have us by them when there is a crisis. But we have an inkling that this calm person is not the whole of us and that we are not averse at times to playing the 'calming influence' role while a different sort of reality in us looks on.

Other people say, 'You are just like your father', and we can see not only the physical likeness but also the way our characters match. It is unquestionable that there is a genetic affinity between our parents and ourselves, but a part of us may wish to rebel against the stereotyping that people practise upon us. 'I don't want to be like my father. I want to be different', we say with little idea how we might set about it.

We are all of us aware too that we are strongly affected by the environment we are brought up in. 'What can you expect,' they say of us, 'coming from a home like that?' But 'a home like that' will sometimes produce two children utterly unlike in their feelings for life and their approach to it. 'I'm quite different from my sister,' we say firmly. There is no rational way that we can explain why one child grows up so radically different from the other.

The usual handy explanations about our natures, our heredity or our environment for feeling the way we discover we do are in no way sufficient. There is a restlessness in us which touches deeper levels. We feel more responsible than these reasons give us credit for. If we are feeling bad, perhaps for no reason that we can put our finger on, we excuse ourselves or, sometimes with great harshness, judge ourselves. If our feelings are normally good, we wonder why we have been so favoured, how soon the blessing might vanish away and whether it is at all fair.

Many of our feelings seem to have an unconnected air. Of course there are immediately understandable ones too, the ones that give us at least a small foothold in the real world. If we win £10,000 in a newspaper competition we can understand ourselves feeling elated. If we suffer the death of our spouse we . expect to feel hurt, angry and abandoned. But aside from these rare and absorbing events, feelings appear to arrive like unannounced guests. We discover we have a vague sense of unease, an incipient depression or a desire to be really violent and we say, 'I don't know why I feel like this.' We cannot find any connection with what is happening around us or what has recently happened.

At other times feelings leap upon us, like children jumping out of a cupboard to frighten us. We attend some community festivity and expect to pass through it with our accustomed sobriety, and we suddenly find ourselves entering into the spirit of the day and dancing the mayor's wife round the square. 'I can't think what got into me,' we say. 'I didn't know I could be like that.' Often the moment of recognition of our behaviour is the moment that sobriety returns and we withdraw our hand from the lady's waist, go pink with embarrassment and apologize.

We may already be becoming aware of two themes that underlie all these uncertainties. As my argument progresses we shall find each of them frequently engaging our attention, so I shall do no more than raise them at this stage.

The first is the recognition that we have a strange capacity to stand aside from ourselves and to observe ourselves in the process of feeling. We are all familiar with this fact of self-reflection. It is one of the major characteristics that differentiates us from all other known creatures. Yet the process sometimes occurs in the midst of the most intense feelings in a way which throws doubt upon their reality. We are appalled that there is an apparently unfeeling part of us which is able to observe an unquestionably emotional experience of ours with a dispassionate curiosity which borders on the immoral.

I recall a woman telling me, for example, that at the very moment she heard that her child had died and she collapsed into an uncontrollable distress which she neither then nor ever later saw as anything but a genuine and loving grief, at that moment, she told me, a small part of her looked on and remarked coolly, 'That's a good show you're putting on, my dear.' What sort of scoundrel is such a spectator? We may perhaps properly, and often do, berate ourselves for not feeling as compassionate as we ought in the face of the misery of others. Whatever we know we ought to feel about their adversity in fact we find ourselves indifferent. But how is it possible for any part of us to be indifferent to an emotional impulse of our own which we should rightly expect to engage every part of us?

The other more important, because more urgently practical, theme that has already surfaced concerns our need, but our incapacity, to change. The Brute family 'changed their name to Nice' and we wish we found it as easy as that. There are few of us that do not wish to find ways of making the better feelings take root in us. We travel round with 'oughts' waiting for us at every corner. They may be the imperious 'oughts' of present authorities – the parents or in-laws who tell us how we are to bring up our children, the church or minister who tells us what sort of conduct God requires from us, the spouse who can raise our conscience's temperature with a single look. Or they may be a more subtle set of demands which keep crawling up to the surface from within ourselves and whose origin we cannot fathom. Even if we are able to bring some sort of order out of these claims upon us so that we know which is, and which is not, a sensible or attainable end to achieve, we rarely know how to begin to effect any sort of change in them.

If we have reached the conclusion that we ought to feel kinder towards our neighbour, for instance, how do we bring about such a change in our feelings? If we find that, in practice, we can do nothing whatever about our feeling for her, does this mean that the reality is that our feelings control us and we do not control our feelings? And in that event how is it ever possible to do anything about our feelings, or even to be held responsible for them?

As I say, these are difficult questions, easier to ask than to answer, and I shall be returning to them later. Here I would like to continue to raise the issues by giving some examples of contexts in which emotion, or the apparent lack of it, is pronounced. Let me begin with a child, which we all once were. Jane Eyre, aged ten, for some misdemeanour had been locked into a spare room for several hours and night draws on. She imagines that a streak of light outside is a visiting phantom and she becomes panic-stricken.

> My heart beat thick, my head grew hot; a sound filled my ears, which I deemed the rushing of wings; something seemed near me; I was oppressed, suffocated: endurance broke down; I rushed to the door and shook the lock in desperate effort. Steps came running along the outer passage; the key turned, Bessie and Abbot appeared.
> 'Miss Eyre, are you ill?' said Bessie.
> 'What a dreadful noise! It went quite through me!' exclaimed Abbot.
> 'Take me out! Let me go into the nursery!' was my cry.
> 'What for! Are you hurt! Have you seen something?' again demanded Bessie.
> 'Oh, I saw a light, and I thought a ghost would come.' I now got hold of Bessie's hand, and she did not snatch it from me.
> 'She has screamed out on purpose', declared Abbot, in some disgust.

Jane's stern aunt and foster-mother, Mrs Reed, now appeared on the scene and takes sides with Bessie and Abbot.

> 'O aunt, have pity! Forgive me! I cannot endure it – let me be punished some other way. I shall be killed if – '
> 'Silence! This violence is most repulsive;' and so, no doubt, she felt it. I was a precocious actress in her eyes: she sincerely looked on me as a compound of virulent passions, mean spirit and dangerous duplicity.[2]

The invariable experience of our childhoods is the growing surge of powerful, urgent and only half-understood emotions, and the inhibitions that are placed upon them by our elders. Jane feels both intense anger because she has been punished, as she believes unjustly, and a desperate fear in the face of unknown forces about her, some of which forces of course are the strengths of those very adults she is in conflict with, re-appearing in a mysterious form. Her anger and fear are interpreted by the adults about her variously as a disease ('Miss Eyre, are you ill?'), pig-headedness ('She has screamed out on purpose'), depravity ('This violence is most repulsive'), self-interest ('mean spirit') and histrionics ('I was a precocious actress in her eyes'). Small wonder she felt isolated and hurt, as all of us used sometimes to feel when we were young, particularly when nobody seemed to understand how we felt inside and everybody seemed to misinterpret our feelings blindly or maliciously.

We never had any control either over the arrival of the emotions that we discovered we possessed when we were children. We felt intensely tied up in a mixture of love and hate for our parents. We felt jealous of our brothers and sisters because we had not yet learnt that love could be, and had to be, shared around. We felt deliriously happy when everything came out as we hoped and angry when we were deprived of the rights, freedoms and possessions we instinctively felt were properly ours.

Adults, whether or not they themselves were comfortable with an emotional life, gave a quite unexpected prominence to feelings in their relationship with us. It was of no consequence whether they were or were not able to express their love, to put their arms around us or to talk with us about their own emotional life. They still told us that we should not feel angry, resentful, ill-natured or unforgiving and demanded that we should feel loving and grateful, happy and nice. Our emotional world was dictated to us in a welter of 'musts' and 'shoulds' and 'oughts' which by no means accorded with the realities of what we felt inside. It was sometimes as if we were all living on the brink of a cataclysm. If once the storm was allowed to break unspeakable consequences would follow. It was of the utmost importance therefore that potentially damaging emotions should be dampened down and inhibited. As Mrs Reed said to Jane Eyre, 'It is my duty to show you that tricks will not answer ... it is only on condition of perfect submission and stillness that I shall liberate you.'

So we grew up balanced, and often torn, between two demands, that of our feelings and that of our parents or other carers. The first could not be denied without doing violence to our very nature, the second could only be denied at the cost of our parents' sanctions, which were sometimes bewildering, and at the risk of losing their love. We set to therefore to reconcile these two demands as best we could.

Bound to our parents, particularly to our mother, from the moment of conception, our most crucial task was to ensure that we retained that security and love. We needed to belong, to have and to keep the people who gave meaning to our existence. This feeling was at first completely instinctive, but soon arose the capacity to test out that love against the dawning awareness of ourselves as individuals. We felt we wanted to go through the fence at the bottom of the garden but would they still love us if we did? We didn't want to eat our lunch and somehow the very intensity of our mother's desire that we should eat it increased our determination not to, though had she not been so insistent we were in all honesty feeling quite hungry.

I remember our son, aged about three, disappearing into the garden one summer's day. After a time we missed him and went hunting and calling him, fears for his safety quickly gagging our throats. Quite twenty minutes later he emerged grinning from behind a bush where he had been completely still and well-hidden, and was welcomed back with scolds and hugs. He had been testing out both the possibility of being separated from us and the strength of our love and our acceptance of him on his return.

At this early pre-rational stage, even though we needed to try out our personal strength, it was quite exceptionally important that we should not lose love. For there is strong evidence that children have an exaggerated notion of their own power and can easily assume that the loss of a parent, through death, divorce or even through a permanent indifference, is the direct result of some thoughtless expression of their own feelings. I have myself talked with adults who, reflecting years later on such an early loss, have come to a realization that they have always felt guilty about it in the unconscious belief that 'it was my fault'.

As older children, when we began thinking and judging for

ourselves, we might have reflected, for example, that there has to be some limit to the expression of our feelings of hatred and anger. We could not hit out at everybody who hurt us partly because they were capable of hitting back and might have been stronger than we were in physique or character but also because of the old problem of losing affection. We needed their love and we would therefore put some embargo upon the expression of our anger for fear either that they might harm us in return or that we might drive them away. Or again in the times of our distress we might have taken the tears of our loneliness up to our bedroom out of sight. We would not have wanted to throw open doubt upon the love of those who cared for us by showing them that we were upset nor would we have wished to risk an indifference to, or a rejection of, our misery.

In some such way did most of us stumble through our childhood, caught between our feelings and the authorities that surrounded us.

There was the turmoil of our emotions on the one hand which we somehow identified with our personhood. I say 'somehow' because it was not at all clear to us in what precise respects our feelings made us our own selves and nobody else. It was not always to do with the greater passions, during which, as I have noted, we often discover a wry observer within ourselves. It was rather the certainty that if we felt something then it was we who felt it and nobody else and therefore our feelings were peculiarly our own. Outside us lived the other authorities who made many claims upon us and upon whom, in turn, we were in no doubt that we wished to make claims of our own. These authorities hedged our feelings round with prohibitions, some of which we recognized were for our own safety but all of which at one time or another, consciously or unconsciously, we deeply resented.

It is not by accident that a book about the emotions started with an infants' story, proceeded with an account of the experience of a ten-year-old girl and has developed into a discussion about our early lives at home. It is because those early experiences are, without exception, the formative years of all our lives and we all have to come to terms with that fact sooner or later.

We have inherited from our parents certain genes which, in general terms, have given us unalterable characteristics, like ginger hair or close-set eyes. This is a simple physical transaction between our parents and ourselves. They have also given us a complex of feelings, a psychological shape which will also be with us all our lives but which, unlike the genes, we have some subsequent opportunity of reshaping in order to conform to our new emerging selfhood. This selfhood is to some degree determined by our early experiences, and by the accidents that befell our lives at that time, but is also something fresh to the world. We need to deny neither the reality of each one of us as a unique individual nor the undoubted fact that we have been moulded by those who had care of us when we were young.

It is this tension that dogs us all our days. There is the person we are or into which we sense we are capable of being transformed, and there is another person into which our earliest authorities have shaped us and from which we spend much time and energy trying to escape. For even when we have freed ourselves from every immediate entanglement with our parents, in later life we are constantly making relationships which reflect their authority over us, negatively or positively. Indeed it must be true to say that any later authority we either have to suffer, like teachers or policemen, or we choose, like spouses or political parties, will yield clues to what was happening to us when we were children, to the sort of shape we grew up in.

Our membership of the church is one of those authorities and one of those clues. However we have arrived in the church, in some sense it holds sway over us. We expect it to give guidance, to establish doctrine and to lay down ground rules for its adherents.

For some people, those who may be content not to pay too close an attention to their emotional lives, this is enough. The church, and sometimes its ministers, stand *in loco parentis*. For others new battles have to be undertaken against this new authority. Their individualism, which is somehow bound up with the feelings and experiences which nobody else can take away from them, demands confrontation. Most of us perhaps hover uncertainly between those poles, grumbling about the church's ministers, agonizing in a muddled sort of way about the difficulties that the church throws up for us, and in the end deciding, quietly and privately, how we shall act religiously.

All authorities subsequent to our childhood have the same troubles with us as our parents discovered. They cannot allow us to act so individually that their power is undermined, and, since the emotions are the prime source of independence, the authorities are bound to attempt to exercise some sort of control over the expression of our feelings.

Unhappily, the church throughout its history, for reasons that we shall look at in the next chapter, has usually seen the development of Christian individuals in terms of a passive acceptance of its own authority. The church has had, as we shall see, a deep-seated fear of individual emotions. Feelings are by nature capricious, aberrant and therefore dangerous. Feelings are either sinful or fraught with the possibility of sin and are best avoided. We hear the same voice echoing in the church as we heard in our childhood. 'Just don't you dare ...' 'What would your mother say?' 'Now say you're sorry.' 'I told you so.'

Certain emotions, however, the church has been able to come to terms with, usually because they are expressed within its own terms of reference. If emotion is expressed religiously or can be seen to have a religious outcome, virtually any extravagance is acceptable. And since the extravagant will often give clues about the humdrum it might now be helpful to look at some examples of emotion which the church usually permits.

William James in *The Varieties of Religious Experience* tells the story of a freethinking French Jew who, in 1842, in a way that stretched the Frenchman's own credulity to the limit and with an accompanying storm of emotion, was converted one half-hour to Roman Catholicism. There were few predisposing conditions except that his brother had been converted and had become a Roman Catholic priest. He writes in his own words:

I entered the church myself to look at it. The church of San Andrea was poor, small and empty; I believe that I found myself there almost alone ... I can only remember an entirely black dog which went trotting and turning before me as I mused. In an instance the dog had disappeared, the whole church had vanished, I no longer saw anything ... or more truly I saw, O, my God, one thing alone.

Heavens, how can I speak of it? Oh no! Human words cannot attain to expressing the inexpressible. Any description, however sublime it might be, could be but a profanation of the unspeakable truth.

I was there prostrate on the ground, bathed in tears, with my heart beside itself, when M.B. called me back to life. I could not reply to the questions which followed from him one upon the other. But finally I took the medal which I had on my breast, and with all the effusion of my soul I kissed the image of the Virgin, radiant with grace, which it bore. Oh, indeed, it was She! It was indeed She! (what he had seen had been a vision of the Virgin).

I did not know where I was: I did not know whether I was Alphonse or another. I only felt myself changed and believed myself another me; I looked for myself in myself and did not find myself. In the bottom of my soul I felt an explosion of the most ardent joy ... How came I to this perception? I can answer nothing save this, that on entering the church I was in darkness altogether, and on coming out of it I saw the fulness of light ... Better than if I saw them, I *felt* these hidden things; I felt them by the inexpressible effects they produced in me. It all happened in my interior mind; and those impressions, more rapid than thought, shook my soul, revolved and turned it, as it were, in another direction.[3]

A modern evangelist, R. A. Torrey, at the other end of the ecclesiastical spectrum, describes a similar sort of emotional experience more shortly like this:

Suddenly it was just as if I had been knocked out of my chair on to the floor, and I lay upon my face, crying, 'Glory to God! Glory to God!' I could not stop. Some power, not my own, had taken possession of my lips and my whole person ... I had never shouted before in my life but I could not stop.[4]

It is a shock suddenly to turn stories like these. Some of us may have gone through a conversion experience but few have been as dramatic as those and most of our lives anyway are not lived at that kind of level. Is *that* what religious experience is all about? we ask. Are we really expected to feel like that if we are to be judged truly religious? If we have only rarely, or have never, had that kind of experience does that throw doubt upon the authenticity of our religious faith? Is that what 'feelings' mean in a religious context?

Some religious groups would answer 'Yes' to all those questions. There is a number of religious people who not only seek to bring everybody to a point of crisis so that they have the clarity of a 'before and after' conversion behind them but who thereafter seek to raise and to keep the emotional temperature at a heightened level. The examples of this are so common these days and so frequently shown and written about that it is unnecessary to give further instances. We just need to note at this stage that this is becoming less and less a minority view of religion and of religion's relationship with emotion. Religious people are seeking emotional experience, frequently in an extravagant fashion.

There is nothing mysterious about this. What happened to Jane Eyre is probably the sort of thing that once happened to us. Not often but occasionally. Our everyday feelings may have been commonplace but none of us has lacked those moments of passion in our youth which have been immediately, and maybe rightly, inhibited and therefore never fully released. It is not amazing that we should accept with open arms a subsequent invitation to release that which has been shackled for so long. Nor do we need for the moment to make judgments about this behaviour, whether it is a right or a wrong way to practise our faith, whether God is always at work in such circumstances. All I am inviting you to do at the moment is to reflect upon the process. Leaving on one side for the time whether such a question is irrelevant in a religious context, what from a human point of view could be happening? A short examination of the factors involved in the two accounts of religious experience we have before us might help us to illuminate this question.

Both men quickly found themselves flat on the floor as if God had struck them down. 'I was there prostrate on the floor.' 'Just as if I had been knocked out of my chair.' Abasement before the mystery of God may have put them there but it was as if their bodies were no longer under their control. Each appears to have become almost, but not quite, insensible and we begin to wonder what part their physical needs played in their conversion. We should beware of dismissing their experience even if such a connection were to be suspected. The religious too easily under-estimate the part the physical plays in religion, or view it pejoratively.

For each man the change was uninduced in the sense that neither apparently had any hand in bringing the experience about. It was done to them, not by them, and the force that did it arrived mysteriously. This is one of the most potent factors in all such religious experiences, that the change which we are ever confused as to how to bring about, is accomplished for us. We are changed. We shall be looking later at whether we are bound hopefully to await the arrival of the change-bringer or whether there are any methods of helping change along for ourselves.

The change brought something completely new. This was the wonder of it for each man. They talk about it a little differently. Torrey talks of 'some power not my own' which 'had taken possession of my life'. He was taken over and yet it was a take-over of 'my whole person'. He was still seen to be Torrey yet felt himself different. The Frenchman 'believed myself another me; I looked for myself and did not find myself.' His companion had no doubt whose shoulder he was shaking on the church floor but the man himself 'did not know whether I was Alphonse or another'. They were altered people and were bowled over by the change. How ardently did we clench our small hands together when we were young and pray to God that we might be different! And sometimes it happened. Nor do we need to look that far back over the years to know that there have been changes in us, that we have become at least a litle new, with or without the aid of experiences like those of Torrey and Alphonse.

These events were undoubtedly both religious ('Glory to God! Glory to God!') and charged with emotion ('Better than if I saw them, I *felt* those hidden things'). We should not be afraid to look at another wholly secular emotionally laden experience, this time of an adult, to see if we can find any parallels. So here is an account, from William James again, of a General Skobeleff. He is speaking of his experience of war and the excitement of danger:

> I believe that my bravery is simply the passion and at the same time the contempt of danger. The risk of life fills me with an exaggerated rapture. The fewer there are to share it, the more I like it. The participation of my body in the event is required to furnish me an adequate excitement. Everything intellectual appears to me to be reflex; but a meeting of man to man, a duel, a danger into which I can throw myself headforemost, attracts me, moves me, intoxicates me. I am crazy for it, I love it, I adore it ... When I throw myself into an adventure in which I hope to find it, my heart palpitates with the uncertainty; I could wish at once to have it appear and yet

to delay. A sort of painful and delicious shiver shakes me; my entire nature runs to meet the peril with an impetus that my will would in vain try to resist.[5]

It would require the alteration of only a very few words for this story to be transformed into an account of a religious experience of the nature we have been considering. There is the same sense of excitement, even frenzy, the same desire to sacrifice everything for a single cause, the same sense of integration achieved or imminently achievable. Make God the object in place of danger and we could be back with Alphonse and Torrey.

Some of the themes are similar. The General, in rather an odd phrase, requires 'the participation of my body in the event'. He knows that his commitment requires the whole of him, though there is a discrediting of the rational part of him ('everything intellectual appears to me to be reflex') which is not infrequently characteristic of those who discover an emotional religion. He flings himself into danger in spite of himself, he is not responsible for it ('an impetus that my will would in vain try to resist'). There is a mysterious outside force which first makes his every nerve tingle with anticipation and then impels him forward. And although the danger is similar each time and the General goes into battle anticipating what will happen, his expectations are congruent with those of millions of religious people who keep seeking a recrudescence of their first love in further emotional excitement.

Emotions of this nature then, bearing the same marks everywhere, are recognizable wherever they appear and whatever their object. They engage the whole person, body and soul. They bring to light a crisp reality which leaves an observer in no doubt that something is happening. They produce excitement and a certain integration of the spirit. They happen without the will of the subject; the change is caused by forces outside the person, though the co-operation of the subject is assumed. They are always in danger of swamping rationality.

In all of this they bear the same marks as those of our common experiences where the emotions are sharply focussed and where the cause and effect are manifestly joined. Thus the experiences of mourning, of falling in love and of failure or success in some immediate venture all fall under this heading. 'O Lord, isn't life marvellous?' we say or, 'O Lord, I can't bear it.'

What is by no means so obvious is what relation these phenomena bear to those other troubling but much vaguer emotions which, though caused by strange outside forces and affecting our whole being, yet bring more darkness than light, have an opaque relationship to reality and fragment rather than integrate the spirit. To these matters we shall need to return.

One further example will serve to complete this introduction, a story much less extreme in some ways than those we have been considering. The extremes sometimes offer us a broader hint about reality than the ordinary nor should we underestimate the great weight of unpractised feelings in us which are waiting their day. It would be surprising if most of us have not already felt some spark of recognition even amongst the singularities thus far described. Yet most of the time we live lives altogether more mundane.

So let me turn finally to talk of Hensley Henson who ended a prestigious ministry in the Church of England as Bishop of Durham between 1920 and 1939. We know a great deal about him and his ministry because he is one of the few bishops who have set their minds down in autobiographical form. His autobiography runs to over seven hundred pages and quotes extensively from a journal he kept all his working life. We should therefore know a great deal about how he felt. The strange thing is that in all those words, though we learn a lot about what he thought and said and how he practised his ministry, though we gain a fascinating insight into the workings of an established church over a period of some fifty years, we learn practically nothing at all about his feelings. His wife, for example, who lived and worked at his side throughout and whom he seems to have relied upon, once received a compliment at the end of their time in Hereford which he, most unusually, records. It was said of her, 'She will be greatly missed by a host of friends in city and country.' His only comment is a distant, 'I think this is probably true.'[6]

The reasons for this sort of restraint he does himself refer to when he is talking about Frank Buchman's Oxford Movement, a charismatic group of the time. He writes in a letter:

Temperamentally I dislike emotional religion. One of the continuing trials of my life is the almost physical repugnance which I feel towards 'corybantic Christianity', a repugnance

which has betrayed me more than once into language that was
unwise and probably unfair ... On the whole (he concludes) I
suppose that the attitude of Gamaliel is as much as can be
required from me.[7]

Now Henson was a man of very strong opinions, many of
them well ahead of his time. It is quite spellbinding, for instance,
to read of his views when he was Canon of Westminster about
the virgin birth and the resurrection which reflect so closely
those of his successor as Bishop of Durham seventy years later.
He wrote in 1914:

> Why should I concern myself *religiously* with an alleged
> resuscitation, even though supported by a seemingly inexplic-
> able 'empty tomb'? The modern world reeks with prodigies,
> supported by circumstantial evidence in plenty, and (what is
> lacking in this case) by the evidence of eye-witnesses.[8]

Such convictions were no more popular then than now, but
Henson stated them with a rigid honesty, an acute intelligence
and a fine oratory – but, so far as he allows us to see, without any
passion.

I relate that at some length not in order to reassure that there
are people who can survive without emotion. On the contrary.
For what happened with Henson was that his ministry was
surrounded throughout by a veritable storm of passion of which
he was the source. It was somehow because he related his views
so dispassionately that his opponents rampaged so violently.
There was a displacement of the emotions, a reappearance
in another place of feelings that were kept firmly in check
elsewhere.

We shall see later how easily this comes about in all our
relationships. Emotions can never be made to vanish once they
have arrived. They have to be dealt with one way or another. If
they are, for any one of a dozen reasons, refused, if we will not
accept them as our own, then they will establish themselves
elsewhere and revive in unexpected forms.

Now we may all have reached the end of this chapter with a
sense of despair that we shall ever be able to bring order out of
such chaos, and there is some justification for such gloom.

There is no easy way through the chaos of our emotions. They
are by their very nature disruptive, uncouth and complex.

Those of you who have already travelled some of the paths that this book records will know how painful, how confusing and what hard work that journey can be. We are dealing with the very foundation of our existence as human beings and it is hard to stand aside from ourselves far enough to see clearly where we are going and where we should go. All I am attempting to do in this book is to offer some clues about a journey which I am myself of course still travelling.

It seems a little curious at first sight but I believe most strongly that it is our thinking about our emotional life that needs to be addressed first of all. I do not in the least mean to imply that emotions yield to a rational approach. We have all met far too many men and women who live their lives through their minds and are cold as fish. No, it is just that I am convinced that we are so often 'wrong-headed', in the literal sense, in our approach to the emotions and that the first course, before we move a single step, is to become 'right-minded', or anyway as right-minded as is necessary to begin the journey.

The next chapter then is a sort of ecclesiastical extension of this one. I examine how the Bible cheerfully takes part in the chaos of our emotions yet how the church, almost from the beginning, could not cope with Jesus' radical approach to human relations and quickly found ways of suppressing the threatening impulse of the emotions.

Chapter 3 is very central to an understanding of what I am after. It is my experience that many of us have been led to believe that emotions in themselves have a moral content. It is bad to be angry, bad to hurt people, bad to be jealous, bad to be disobedient. It is good, however, to love people, good to feel happy, good even to feel sad at times. I shall argue that on the contrary all our emotions are morally quite neutral. We are induced to think of them as good and bad not by God but by various external authorities. There is enormous release from a primal guilt when we understand that it is only our handling of our emotions once they have arrived that leads us into the moral field. We need to learn to love our emotions, all our emotions, as we love ourselves.

Chapters 4 and 5 are about love and anger respectively, in which I attempt to work through that principle in the areas of two emotions which are central to all our lives. What is the difference between feeling love and doing love and where does sexuality fit in? Anger can be both freeing and destructive. How do we make our anger free?

Chapter 6 looks at some clear, practical steps we can take to come to terms with our feelings and, under the heading of the Fact and the Feeling, attempts a more rational examination of what might be happening in that process.

Chapter 7 takes up this same theme in terms of the oft-suggested control of the emotions, a concept that I find less than helpful, as I try to show.

In the last chapter I return to the church, seeking effective methods of bringing real emotion, and therefore real vitality, back into the mainstream of the church's life.

2

Bible and Church

If there is one thing that is quite clear when we open the pages of the Bible it is that we do not enter upon a world of quiet and devoted spirituality. We do not find ourselves, as with so much of the world's great religious literature, transported away from the cares and troubles of the earth to a peaceable place where God supposedly reigns in tranquility and whither we are bidden to strive to join him. Rather we discover that we are reading about a people and a God who emotionally appear to be as shockingly chaotic, wayward and even immoral as we know ourselves to be. In a great many ways the Bible makes our hair stand on end.

That realization can be something of a relief. It is reassuring to find that the Christian's holy book shares much of the inner disturbance and some of the defencelessness which we experience. But there is another side of us which is scandalized that a book which is avowedly religious and therefore supposedly good should be, so to speak, so little above us. So we search earnestly for the uplifting passages and, aided and abetted by many of the churches' lectionaries, pass swiftly over those which war with our better aspirations. The Holy Bible, like so many of our emotions, is not holy enough for us.

The Old Testament is disturbingly frank, for example, about the relationship between men and women both when it goes well (read the Song of Songs) or when it is primitive (Samson, Judg.13 ff.) and destructive (Tamar and Amnon, II Sam.13).

The violence which we sometimes surprise in ourselves is in the
Old Testament a part of everyday life. Very strict laws bear what
seem to us disproportionate punishments (a man who gathers
sticks on the sabbath day is stoned to death, Num. 15, 32 – 6;
blasphemy is also a capital offence, Lev. 24. 13–16); unbelievable
barbarity is inflicted in the Lord's name ('Blessed is the man who
takes your babies and smashes them against the rocks' Ps. 137.
88): Esther, in a sorry tale of treachery and deceit, crowns all by
ensuring that her adversary is hanged (Esth. 7).

There is a fanatical nationalism which leads to the forcible
breaking-up of marriages (Ezra 9 and 10) alongside a care for
the foreigners who take up residence in Israel (Lev. 19. 33–4).
Ecclesiastes encourages a sort of saloon bar cynicism which we
occasionally sink to while many of the psalms touch deep roots in
us of mystical communion with God. Everywhere we look we
find echoes of our own behaviour – constancy and betrayal,
sexual attraction and marital deception, benevolence and callous-
ness, brutality and tenderness – and the better habits are not
uniformly commended nor the worse always condemned.

Israel's God shares in this turbulence, is even at times subject
to it. The Bible talks shamelessly of God's anger: 'I will take
revenge on my enemies and punish those who hate me. My
arrows will drip with their blood, and my sword will kill all who
oppose me' (Deut. 32. 41 f.) and makes no judgment upon him
when he coolly decides: 'I will wipe out all these people I have
created, and also the animals and the birds, because I am sorry
that I made any of them' (Gen. 6. 7).

He causes a woman to drop a millstone on Abimelech's head
in order to 'pay him back' for having disposed of his seventy
brothers (Judg. 9) and exacts from the Israelites obedience for
the destruction of the total population of the city of Jericho
(Josh. 6). When Jacob deceives his father Isaac, tricks Esau out
of his birthright and his blessing, and hoodwinks his equally
fraudulent father-in-law Laban, God tells him, 'I am with you. I
will bless you and give you many descendants because of my
promise to my servant Abraham' (Gen. 26. 23). He gets into an
absurd argument with Abraham, haggling over the number of
righteous people who might inhibit the destruction of Sodom
(Gen. 18) and he seems curiously uncertain how to handle
Satan's needling of him over Job's righteousness (Job 1 and 2).

The New Testament is no less a record of confused allegiances and strong emotions, positive and negative. St Paul, for instance, magnificent missionary though he be, is constantly involved in intense relationships, violent quarrels and self-justification. He castigates St Peter for his chicken-heartedness over the admission of the Gentiles to the church (Gal. 2) and the Corinthian church for their blatant acceptance of immoral behaviour (1 Cor. 4 etc). He flings his arms around the Ephesians on the seashore and weeps bitterly with them because they will not see each other again (Acts 20. 36–8). Wherever he travels and whoever he is with he is dogged by enthusiasms and antagonisms.

The days of the ministry of Jesus, too, are characterized by surging crowds, hungry for bread, for miracles and for further teaching from this strange, authoritative man, and by near riots as the enthusiasm and excitement of the crowds meets the fury of the religious authorities. The disciples, volatile in their allegiance, blowing hot and cold, misunderstanding, fomenting internal jealousies, yet have abandoned their entire livelihood for the sake of this new master.

The early church, from the day of Pentecost onwards, sees frenetic scenes of spiritual ecstasy, intense preaching followed by disorder, arrest and punishment, sharp divisions between Christians who are not yet quite sure what a Christian is, and a love for one another which is quite new to the world but which makes it difficult to know how to handle the old doctrines of exclusiveness.

This almost random selection of events from the two testaments is meant to do no more than to help us to see that, whether we welcome it or not, the Bible shares our emotional turmoils. My view is that there are at least two consequences of this fact which are highly productive for Christian discipleship.

First then I believe we need to understand that because the Bible shares our experiences and because Israelite and Christian people and their God have demonstrably felt what we feel, then we can, now and always, have confidence in the document that lays the foundation of our faith. Our emotions are an absolutely direct route into the experiences and the events that the Bible records. The emotional confusion of the Bible is disturbing but it is also our liberation.

For it is by no means easy these days to have confidence that the Bible is to be relied upon. Modern scholarship in its attempts to understand the Bible has tended rather to undermine it for those who have neither the time nor the skill to give to the task. Authorship of various books is in doubt and we cannot say as surely as we used to, 'Jesus said ...' We want to answer the question, 'Is the Bible really true?' with a resounding Yes! but find ourselves slipping in the shale of relativity. What sort of truth do we mean? Historically accurate or true to what we experience? Nor will the cultural problems go away. If it is bad enough for us on our foreign holidays to try to come to terms with the odd customs of other countries how can we be expected to make sense of a middle-eastern culture of several thousand years ago? Small wonder that all those Christians who are not prepared to be fundamentalist about the Bible approach it somewhat gingerly, uncertain about their capacity to make it intelligible on their own or about what authority to trust.

The problems raised by modern scholarship cannot be evaded and we will all, if we are wise, make what little headway we can with them. But we do need to know, here with the Bible, that our emotions, and our recognition of emotions, are to be trusted. The Bible is written by human beings and, for much of the time, about human beings, and the one thing we can be certain about is that they had feelings as we have. Anger, love, jealousy, pride, depression were all part of their experience as they are part of ours. Their reasons for feeling in a certain way may today strike us as strange. For example, it is not quite clear why the Lord should have accepted Abel's offering and not Cain's and we have some small sympathy with Cain's objection to such favouritism. But his anger is crystal clear to us, as is his desire for revenge and, after the murder, his subsequent guilty despair (Gen. 4). We can feel what he felt because we know what such emotions are like.

This is not to say that we shall not sometimes misinterpret biblical emotions just as we misinterpret those of our families and friends, and in all our relationships honest observation, acquired knowledge, careful thought and lots of talking are indispensable to an accurate interpretation of feelings. But experience of those feelings is direct, and it needs to be said that our access to the Bible in this respect is also direct and is to be trusted.

The other consequence which arises out of the marrying of the Bible's emotions with our own leads us much more deeply into the problems that emotion raises, and always has raised, for the church. Perhaps the simplest way of putting the dilemma is to ask the question, 'What are we permitted to feel?'

We are accustomed to making judgments upon our own and others' feelings. If we have a settled rage against somebody and no amount of praying seems to alter it one whit we blame ourselves or search for excellent reasons why we should not blame ourselves. When we observe a friend of ours who forgives wholeheartedly an outrageous indignity inflicted on her we say what a splendid Christian she is. We judge both the action and the feelings that lie behind the action. We instinctively make the same sort of judgments upon the feelings and the actions of people in the Bible. Ruth is a good character because she acted loyally towards her mother-in-law and people should feel that way (Ruth 1). David had no right to feel attracted to somebody else's wife and it was a jolly good thing that Nathan made him condemn himself out of his own mouth (II Sam 12).

But we have already begun to be aware in our examination of the early development of our emotional lives that we are often caught between the feelings we possess and the people around us who tell us that it is wrong to feel this way or that. My argument for the rest of this chapter is that the church, putting itself in the position of authoritative parent, has rarely allowed Christians as wide a freedom in the expression of their feelings as the Bible gives them. It has used its authority to set rigid limits of control over the emotional lives of its adherents, because it has always been frightened of the emotions, which it believes to be anarchic, undisciplined and possibly the devil's tool for bringing men and women to destruction.

There are judgments to be made, of course. Let us, for instance, grant right away that when in the Bible God is said to be angry or jealous we understand that the writers of those days were less subtle in their use of metaphor, more inclined to build God in the image of man, at the mercy of his emotions. As we read we readily make allowance for this, giving a more sophisticated interpretation of passages where God is too human to be true. Moreover we cannot easily commend what seem to us to be most fearful acts of vengeance. When the prophet Samuel 'hewed Agag to pieces before the Lord' (I Sam. 15. 33) or St Paul delivered 'such a one unto Satan for the destruction of the flesh' (I Cor. 5. 5) the moral susceptibilities of most of us are offended and we condemn both the actions and the feelings that give rise to the actions. In other words there are moralities to be considered as well as emotions and a later chapter will be examining some of the boundaries between morality and emotion, giving consideration to the sort of controls that might be helpful and Christian.

Meanwhile the dilemma is raised most acutely in the teaching and life-style of Jesus because what he says and does is readily open to either a severe or a lenient interpretation. He marries at one and the same time an offensive rigorism with an extreme liberalism and seems to be quite unaware of any incongruity. How can we be expected at the same time both to love our enemies (Matt. 5. 44) and to hate our children (Luke 14. 26)? Let us examine briefly his conflicting views on four topics: aggression, riches, sexuality and love.

In the Sermon on the Mount Jesus is very clear about how we should deal with aggression. Turn it aside, absorb it. 'If anyone slaps you on the right cheek, let him slap your left cheek too. And if someone takes you to court to sue you for your shirt, let him have your coat as well' (Matt. 5.39 f.). He exemplified this at his passion, standing quietly before the chief priests and Pontius Pilate, refusing to answer back, choosing to go to his death. Yet earlier he savaged the ruling religious party without any mercy (Matt. 23) and is never recorded as having a single good word to say about any of them. He took a whip to the traders in the temple (John 2. 15). He told his disciples, 'I did not come to bring peace but a sword. I came to set sons against their fathers, daughters against their mothers' (Matt. 10. 34 f.), and that 'whoever has no sword must sell his coat and buy one' (Luke 22. 36). One of those disciples he chose was a political activist (Simon the Zealot, Luke 6. 15).

Time and again Jesus warned his hearers against riches (Luke 6. 24; 12.15; 16.15 etc), even though for the majority of Jews riches were a clear sign of the blessing of God (cf. Mark 10. 26 where the disciples were staggered to hear him say that it would be extremely hard for the rich to enter the Kingdom). Yet he moved comfortably in rich circles (Zacchaeus, the well-to-do woman who supported him financially Luke 8.3, Simon the Pharisee Luke 7. 36 ff.) and chose a tax collector as another disciple.

In sexual morality he could scarcely have been more rigorist.

Marriage was ordained by God at the beginning of creation and 'man must not separate what God has joined together' (Mark 10.9). Going far beyond any then current interpretation of marriage discipline he said that 'a man who divorces his wife and marries another woman commits adultery against her' (Mark 10.11). He appears to have commended the practice of men being castrated 'for the Kingdom of Heaven's sake' (Matt. 19.12). So important was sexual purity that just to want to sleep with another woman was condemnation in itself and it would be better for a man to pluck out his eye or chop off his hand than to fall into any such temptation (Matt. 5. 27 f.). Yet his practice was to mix socially with prostitutes, which made him ritually, as well as morally, unclean, to say that they would enter the Kingdom ahead of the scribes and pharisees (Matt. 21. 31), to proclaim that forgiving others was all that was necessary in order to be forgiven ourselves (Matt. 6. 14 f.) and that love shown by a person was the clearest indication that they had been forgiven (Luke 7. 47). He actively refused to condemn a woman who was caught in the act of adultery (John 8, 1–11), and spent his ministry in an easy and close relationship with a number of women in a manner quite alien to contemporary mores.

We should love our neighbours as ourselves, he declared, and his entire ministry was a demonstration of how that should be done. More than that, we should love our enemies and pray for those who persecute us because we are not to be any more exclusive than God who pours his blessings indiscriminately on good and bad alike. This is the way that we are to become whole people ourselves and an integrated community (Matt. 5. 43–48; the separation of the last verse here from its context has had, as we shall see, the most devastating consequences for the development of Christian spirituality). Yet 'if anyone comes to me and does not hate his father, and mother, and wife, and children, and brothers, and sisters, even his own soul, he cannot be my disciple' (Luke 14. 26; the Good News Bible 'loves me more than he loves . . .' is alas! an euphemism for which there is no textual justification). What is it that makes it necessary to hate our families when the law is the law of love?

At the end of the chapter I shall refer to what I believe underlies this singular polarity of thought and practice in the life and teaching of Jesus. But it is a subject that needs a wider consideration than the terms of this book strictly call for and, as

I say, my main reason for highlighting the ostensible incon-
sistencies at this point is that, historically, it is unquestionable
that the church has used these polarities, one at a time, in order
to commend or condemn a particular Christian life style and to
enforce thereby a particular attitude to the life of the emotions.

For all these words of Jesus made it easy for some of his
disciples, in the grip of one or another psychological or theological persuasion, to attach themselves with enthusiasm to
either his rigorist or his humanist position, to ignore or to
explain away its opposite, and to live their Christian lives either
without discipline or without mercy. Many more of us, aware of
the light and the dark side of our natures, hesitate between the
two poles like elderly people on a traffic island or switch
violently and unsatisfactorily from one side to the other according to our moods or our circumstances. The later books of
the New Testament show these processes aready at work,
though here leaning more and more towards a rigorist position.

I have already introduced St Paul as a man of emotion and
passion. He was also a man with a keen sense of his own
authority, an authority which he felt under threat. In order to
maintain control his attitude to the young churches was often
markedly aggressive. 'When I come next time, I will not spare
you' (II Cor. 13.2). 'But even if we or an angel from heaven were
to preach to you a gospel different from the one you received,
let him be anathema' (Gal. 1.9; 'let him be anathema' are the
words of a formal curse). 'Watch out for the dogs, watch out for
those who do evil things, watch out for the cutters' (Phil 3.2). It is
impossible to read St Paul's epistles without sensing this desire
that his gospel, and his alone, should become the only one
acceptable to the church. We feel the need for self-justification,
the reposing of authority in a man. Jesus talks always of obedience to the Father. St Paul edged towards speaking of obedience
to man, to himself, and begins thereby the process by which a
man's authority keeps in check what others might feel, the
process by which one man's passions are deemed to be sufficient
for the whole.

Jesus' liberalism with regard to money was displayed by his
easy, indifferent acceptance of others' hospitality and generosity
and, so far as we are told, his complete disregard for any
ordering of finance. According to St John he even allowed the
eventual traitor to act as the apostles' treasurer. Money was of no

further concern between those who loved one another. But his rigour lay in his perception that money is extremely dangerous and easily takes up a position as a rival to God (Matt. 6.24, Luke 12.13–21, etc).

St Paul did not follow Jesus down either of these paths. Indeed he adopted a stand which the whole of the church has mostly followed ever since. He was always running into difficulties with money both personally because of the uncertainties that the early church had about how Christian preachers were to be supported, and with respect to the collection for the church in Jerusalem which suffered constantly from deprivations of one sort or another and towards which Paul felt some responsibility. As far as the public collection was concerned he solved these troubles by spending much time raising money for the Jerusalem church, even going so far as to prove his lack of hostility to the mother church by agreeing to take the money there himself.

For his own personal finance, where he was not able to make enough at his own trade of tentmaker, his policy was to persuade one church to support him while he worked in another. His main aim was to distance himself from the money-raising process. 'I didn't charge you a thing when I preached the good news of God to you' (II Cor 11.7). No, it was the other churches that bore the charge. And in any case 'it is not just that I want to receive gifts; rather I want to see profit added to your account' (Phil. 4.17), so it is after all, he implies, for your sake you are raising the money and not mine. Money-raising was not a matter that he cared to get involved in personally. 'Save it up, so that there will be no need to collect money when I come' (I Cor. 16.2). We can hear the echo of ministers down the ages in all of this but we do not hear either Jesus' indifference to money or his claims about its dangers.

It was left to St James to add condemnation to Jesus' rigour. He wrote: 'And now, you rich people, listen to me! Weep and wail over the miseries that are coming upon you. Your riches have rotted away, and your clothes have been eaten by moths. Your gold and silver are covered with rust and this rust will be a witness against you and will eat up your flesh like fire' (James 5.1 ff.).

This stands in stark contrast to the gentle way in which Jesus addressed the rich young man, and to the sadness he shared with him when the young man found that he did after all love money more than God (Mark 10).

It is in the field of sexuality and marriage that St Paul is conspicuously more puritan than his master. Strangely, but in accordance with his usual practice, he rarely uses the words of Jesus which might have been supposed to have strengthened the authority of his words, even though they must have been part of the church's teaching at the time. Rather he seems to rely upon a personal vehemence, a conviction he did not share with Jesus that celibacy is a better state than marriage. I Cor. 7 is a sustained argument to this effect. He himself is celibate and he would prefer everybody else to be the same (v.7). Marriage brings nothing but trouble (v.32). It is a distraction from the service of the Lord and makes a person double-minded (vv.32–34). A widow is well advised not to enter upon matrimony a second time (v.40). Sex is an unfortunate necessity within marriage but is to be preferred to extra-marital relations (v.2) or to frustrated passion (v.9).

Within family life obedience, submission and discipline are to be the watchwords. The husband is responsible for his wife and the wife responsible to her husband. Children do what they are told (Col.3.18–21). We do not hear anywhere of Jesus' relaxed attitude with women and children. Of St Paul's attitude to family life a German theologian wrote decades ago:

> We are regrettably far from the ideal of the Christian household ... The grudging words fall short even of the ideal of family life in classical paganism. Above all there is no recognition of the fact that, even without any high ethical or religious motive, the normal domestic affections ordinarily produce moral results of real importance ... St Paul shows himself ... an ascetic, a hermit, who has never experienced the joys of family life, and perhaps even lacks all capacity for the experience.[1]

So, in spite of the love which Paul can inspire (Phil. 1.8, Acts 20.37) and write about so movingly (I Cor.13), we can already, in comparison with Jesus, detect a hardening of attitudes. As we read his letters we keep company with a man who lives on the edge of his emotions. We feel the passion, the anger often barely suppressed, the feverish desire that his converts shall feel as he feels, the yearning that they shall be as perfect as he wants them to be. It is as if the battles he is fighting with them are a reflection of his own internal struggles, a feeling that spills over into reality in Romans where he talks of 'the desire to do good is in me, but I am not able to do it. I don't do the good I want to do; instead, I do the evil that I do not want to do . . . So I find that this law is at work: when I want to do what is good, what is evil is the only choice I have' (Rom. 7.18–21). His hardness then arises out of the need to be severe with himself, and we shall see later how easily we all fall into that trap.

It is, however, an attitude that other authors in the New Testament are not slow to follow. The author of the Letter of Jude writes: 'Remember Sodom and Gomorrah, and the nearby towns, whose people acted as those angels did and indulged in sexual immorality and perversion. They suffer the punishment of eternal fire as a plain warning to all' (Jude 7).

The writer of the revelation of St John exalts virginity as a sign of the redeemed: 'Of all mankind they are the only ones who have been redeemed. They are the ones who have kept themselves pure by not having sexual relations with women; they are virgins. (Rev 14.3,4; it is interesting how morality is sexually very one-sided in such a passage).

Everywhere harsh action follows harsh words. Consider the following:

> In the letter that I wrote to you I told you not to associate with immoral people. Now I do not mean pagans who are immoral or greedy or are thieves or who worship idols. To avoid them you would have to get out of the world completely. What I meant was that you should not associate with a person who calls himself a brother but is immoral or greedy or worships idols or is a slanderer or a drunkard or a thief. Don't even sit down to eat with such a person. After all it is none of my business to judge outsiders. God will judge them. But should you not judge the members of your own fellowship? As the scripture says, 'Remove the evil man from your group' (1 Cor. 5.9–13).

It is amazing that this sort of attitude should be embraced in the same Christian community which was also circulating stories of the way that Jesus sat at table, with clear deliberation, with exactly the immoral people that Paul recommended his converts to cast out of the community. The gospel that Jesus lived in his ministry was revealed fundamentally in this graciousness to the conspicuously sinful. He consciously turned upside down the conventional wisdom which identified the righteous with the religious. He showed that it was not possible for the truly righteous to be contaminated by association with the unrighteous. 'The last shall be first and the first last.'

It was this blurring of the lines between the righteous and the unrighteous that the church almost immediately repudiated in favour of an ethical rigorism. There is scarcely a hint of Jesus' tolerant compassion outside the four Gospels. The letters of John speak at length about the love that we ought to have for one another, but it is always a love for our 'brother', that is for fellow-members of the church. There is not a single passage in any of the Johannine literature which speaks conclusively of the love that we ought to bear for our neighbour, and even Paul talks only rarely of love for those outside the community (an example is Rom. 13.8–10, but not I Cor. 13 where almost certainly in the context of 'spiritual gifts' he has fellow Christians in mind). The letter to the Hebrews encourages us to welcome strangers into our homes, and to remember those in prison and those who are suffering as if we were there with them (Heb. 13.2,3). But the reference is probably to the church again (note the reference to the 'love of the brotherhood' in verse 1) and earlier we are not encouraged to think of the author as liberal when we read that 'it is impossible to bring (those who have abandoned their faith) back to repent again' (Heb. 6.6) or that 'there is no longer any sacrifice that will take away sins if we purposely go on sinning after the truth has been made known to us' (Heb. 10.26).

It would take us too far from our subject to show how this early calcification of the words of Jesus subsequently led to a formalism and a rigorism, to a tragic pitilessness in the life of the church. Whether it was in the picture of the perfect, redeemed Christian that so many of the earliest Christian writers outside the New Testament depicted, or in the Montanist ravings of a Tertullian ('The sacrifices that are pleasing to God are the torturing of the soul, fastings, a harsh and unpleasing diet, and all the other mortifications that go therewith', *De re.carn.* 8), or in the widespread glorification of the monastic and hence celibate and ascetic state over against the life of the ordinary married Christian in the world, the message was clear.

A line of demarcation is drawn down the middle of the phenomena of life, one side of the frontier being wholly the province of God and the other that of the devil; and all attempts to recognize a middle term, a neutral zone, a bridge or medium of transition between the two are stamped as un-Christian.[2]

The answer the church gave to the question, 'What are we allowed to feel?', then, was 'The less, the better', and it used the words of Jesus to give justification to their advice. 'Be perfect, as your heavenly Father is perfect' (Matt. 5.48), they quoted, and still quote, a phrase which has blighted the lives of millions of Christians these last two thousand years. Apart from the fact that St Luke makes Jesus use the word 'compassionate' in his parallel passage (Luke 6.36), Jesus never intended to talk about the personal idealized state of Christian fantasy. The Greek word in Matthew means 'whole' or 'complete' and the context is that of the way we should all treat each other. 'Anybody can love friends', he says, 'I say we must love enemies too. Our loving must be indiscriminate, as God's is.' What we should be creating each day is the reconciliation of groups and individuals who are naturally antagonistic to one another. As we choose forgiveness, a new community keeps springing up, a present reality and not a distant ideal. This is the 'perfection' that Jesus was talking about.

The very sound of that is antipathetic to the way that the church chose to interpret it, so it is at this point that we must return to the polarities in the teaching of Jesus that I have previously referred to. Why were his words and his actions sometimes at such startling variance with one another? How could he at the same time have both intensified the norms to a virtually unattainable degree and in practice have blunted those same norms? How could he have left himself open to such horrid misinterpretation?

I believe that the clue lies in that 'new creation' which St Paul talks about (II Cor. 5.17; Gal. 6.15). If Jesus saw himself as the begetter of something quite new on the face of the earth, as the bringer of the Kingdom of God, the new message was that God was our Father, which made all people brothers and sisters. To make love the key turned everything upside down.

The poor now became as important as the rich, and the latter were in grave danger because possessions cut them off from people. Riches and position were no longer of any importance in the kingdom of love and there could therefore be a complete indifference to them except in so far as they stood in the way of conversion to the new kingdom when they had to be ruthlessly confronted. Children and women and sinners were now to be welcomed as people of God and, in consequence of their simple lack of expectation of much on earth, were that much more open to hear, and receive, the good news about God. We all needed to become like those children.

God had always intended sexual love for the relationship of marriage where it is to be welcomed and enjoyed. But to see people as sexual objects rather than loving subjects was the antithesis of human loving. On the other hand family relationships, powerfully important as they were as the nexus of love, were also the place where loyalties of great power and intensity arose, loyalties which are always double-edged and can confine as well as liberate. Therefore the family was potentially as great a temptation to set limits to our loving as riches were. It could be another means by which the kingdom was held back, another means of separating people into antagonistic groups. It was not too strong to say that we should 'hate' our families before we learnt to love them again in the new way.

It would be grotesque in the new kingdom that people should indulge in punch-ups with one another. The new kingdom demanded that we should care for one another and turn aside aggression, not so much thereby 'pouring coals of fire on people's heads' as going over to their side and joining them in their disturbing loyalties. Yet such an attitude in itself could be expected to create misunderstanding and aggression, and the reality was that even the new kingdom had to be fought for. Unless we were lucky enough to meet a complaisant opposing power, as Gandhi met the British in India, there would be occasions when we would need to set down our mark and resist its removal.[3]

In some such ways do I see the resolution of the polarization in the words and works of Jesus. But we must not allow such arguments to distract us from the main thrust of our enquiry, which is to recognize the consequences for our emotional life of subsequent misunderstandings of Jesus' position. And what we have seen is that the church quickly came to prefer guilt to forgiveness, exclusion to inclusion, love of the brethren to love of our neighbours, condemnation to kindliness. Contrary voices were of course always making themselves heard and, as we have seen, many of those most disposed to execute judgment were capable of great affection too. But the predominant message was that containment was to be preferred above all else and that therefore the life of the emotions, which was by definition uncontainable, should be suppressed at all costs.

3

Good and Bad Feelings

So far we have seen that our unruly, and often impenetrable, emotions, rooted somehow in our early experiences of life, are hedged about with all kinds of prohibitions and inhibitions. The prohibitions are those of the outside authorities who lay down what we shall and what we shall not feel. The inhibitions are a sort of internal policeman, working to his own unfathomable rules, who monitors our conduct, nods gravely when we do what he approves, ensures that we feel properly guilty when we don't and above all prevents us from undue demonstration of any emotions whatsoever.

We have also seen that religion claims some direction over our emotions. It is exceedingly wary of them, seeing them as one of the main seats of rebellion against itself, but is prepared to countenance them, even in an outlandish form, provided only that they are seen to be moving in the direction of an organized version of itself. Emotions which are conspicuously religious are to be encouraged, otherwise not.

We may have seen this stealthy process of judgment lurking in some religious education that has come our way. We are taught that God loves us and that we are to love God, but the love spoken of is unlike the experience of any of our other loves and we are discouraged from giving any strong expression of it. We are told that we should confess our sins to God and, in some traditions, even to the minister or to the whole fellowship sitting in the seat of God. Often we find that our confession is expected to consist of an open acknowledgment that the dam of our emotions has burst, that we have been angry, lustful, jealous or rude, and the unspoken implication is that we are once again to 'control ourselves'. We are encouraged to join the fellowship of the church where there seems to be a silent rule that everybody shall be nice to one another whatever they happen to feel. The expression of strong feelings, particularly if they are negative, is seen as undermining the group and is to be avoided except in the privacy of some smaller in-group.

We are taught to pray not only with the rest of the church but in the silence of our rooms and of our hearts. We meet there the silence that we successfully avoid in most other areas of our life, a silence in which we hear all too frequently the quiet voice of guilt at the savagery of our emotional life. Our teachers tell us of the principles by which we should live, principles which lay down guidelines for some of our emotions. They are often expressed in negative terms and may or may not coincide with the principles we learnt at home. In either case they often set up in us an internal conflict as we fight to maintain a grip upon our own reality, which by no means necessarily feels bound by the principles proposed.

I mean, the church might tell us that it is wrong to harbour grudges against the brother we grew up with. We are to forgive one another freely, we are told. We quite understand what the church is saying, and in truth we are worn down by a heavy sense of guilt that we cannot bring ourselves to the point of forgiving a person who all our lives has teased and diminished us. Yet he shows absolutely no sign of altering his behaviour towards us, and are we to compound his superiority by asking his forgiveness when the boot should rightly be on the other foot?

All the way through such teaching the good tidings which we accept gladly with our minds and our hearts is often sending a different message to our emotions. We are hearing that our emotions are a treacherous cauldron, waiting for a suitable moment to boil over and get us into hot water with God. Some emotions are good, we are told, but a great many more are bad and the key to handling them all is control.

And thus we arrive at the major task with which this chapter will be mostly concerned. We need to know whether the authorities we have referred to, religious, parental, pedagogic or whatever,

are right in dividing up our feelings and emotions into the
'good' and the 'bad' like that. Are we just bad without remainder
because we have not forgiven our brother? Are some emotions
good and some bad? And which is which?

Most of the authorities will agree that it is, with a few
exceptions, bad to be angry. We ourselves know how destructive
anger can be, especially if we have in the past been at the mercy
of a capricious temper, our own or somebody else's. Anger is
frightening and our own anger frightens us most of all. On the
other hand we recognize uneasily that Jesus was angry, indeed
quite bitter, at times. That is sometimes explained to us as
'righteous anger', and we are unlikely to attain to Jesus' spiritual
purity. But we also may have had the experience of 'blowing our
top' which, far from making us feel bad, has been marvellously
releasing. Anger here has felt good, not bad, and has sometimes
led to a splendid clearing of the air with those who have been at
the sharp end of it.

So what about love? It is good to be loving, we all agree.
Though perhaps not always entirely good. We have known
couples whose love for one another has been for so long
exclusive that they have become selfish in loving. We know how
one love conflicts with another, how the commission of this
particular piece of loving means that somebody else gets kicked
in the teeth. We are uncomfortably aware, even if we only admit
it to ourselves, that our love of those closest to us turns at times
to something close to hate, and we cannot rid our minds of Jesus'
remark that we should hate our family.

It is then certainly bad to be jealous – if it wasn't for the fact
that the Bible is always revelling in the fact that 'I, the Lord, am a
jealous God.' He demands to be exclusive. Don't we all? It is a
simple truth that there will be jealousy between children of the
same family, 'sibling rivalry' as the professionals call it. Can
anything so natural be automatically bad?

It is good to be excited and cheerful and happy. It is bad to be
depressed and mournful. And, heaven knows, there are enough
miserable people around to make us relieved when we meet
some cheery soul who sends us singing on our way with a smile
on our lips. Yet temperament takes a part in the process. Some
people have a fortunate upbringing with a loving, secure home
and others are lumbered with a heart-rending background
which makes us wonder how they have ever coped. It isn't fair to

make moral judgments on people without a full awareness of the facts. Moreover the path to self-awareness is more commonly trodden out of the depths than off the heights.

Whichever way we look we find that there are different ways of looking. It seems to become less and less appropriate to make sweeping judgments about our emotions, designating them unalterably good or bad. It almost seems as if in one sense moral values don't apply where our emotions are concerned, and yet another part of us recognizes that that is absurd because we can each recall occasions, such as when we fell in love or when we were unspeakably hurtful, which we have no doubt had a purity of goodness or badness about them.

So let us suppose for the moment that it is right to call one emotion good and another bad. We then have to ask: Who in practice is deciding? Who is making the judgment about a particular emotion and its goodness or badness? How do we know? Perhaps it will be simplest if we look at the issues in terms of a typical emotion, let us say jealousy. Is jealousy bad or good and how do we know?

We have to say first that either somebody tells us that jealousy is good or we experience it for ourselves or it is a combination of our experiences and somebody else's teaching.

When we were children we were probably told firmly that jealousy was bad. Parents have that sort of authority and nothing that we felt was going to make any difference. When we grew up the responsibility for deciding such an issue became ours and perhaps what we hoped might have come about was that we would have taken carefully into consideration what our parents used to say, what our church teaches and what we were told by our conscience or by God in our times of prayer and then we would have made a decision about it. That is the sort of steps that the rational man takes. 'There's nothing wrong with jealousy', we might have decided or, 'Jealousy really is bad.'

Unfortunately it is unlikely that we ever did take such rational steps or that it would have been as easy as that if we had. For in practice we discover that the emotions war with the rational man.

We work our way splendidly through a series of mental processes and arrive at a satisfactory conclusion when wham! we abruptly discover that, in spite of the fact that we have decided, for instance, that there is nothing wrong with jealousy, we remember our sister, the favoured one in the family. Jealousy comes pouring in because she was so loved, and at the same time we become aware that we feel painfully guilty about our jealous feelings as if jealousy was wrong after all.

As if that irrationality wasn't bad enough, when we look further we discover that it is not just a matter of a conflict between our minds and our feelings, there is a veritable civil war going on in our emotions as well. What do we mean when we say, 'I said to myself' or 'I was beside myself with rage'? Who are all these people who seem to have taken up residence inside us? I know I have referred previously to the ability we have to stand aside from ourselves, but this is ridiculous! We seem to speak with several voices one after another or even all at the same time.

At this point it may be helpful to be reminded of those childhood experiences I referred to in the first chapter. Some of the voices that arise out of our inner selves are the left-over voices of the past skulking in our shadows. They are not exactly the voices of our parents, though they will be part of it, but rather vague forces we cannot quite identify which appear to have the power to prevent us acting in ways that other parts of us would like to or compel us to move in directions a part of us resists.

It is all to do with the way we have come into the world and the influence of those who were closest to us in those early days, naturally as a rule our father, mother, brothers and sisters. One way to think of it is to consider a small seed we might plant in our garden. Whether the seed grows to full maturity, as magnificently formed as the picture on the outside of the packet, depends upon many factors. The quality of the seed itself is at issue and that depends upon the quality of the mother-plant it comes from. The seed needs adequate quantities of water, light, nourishment and space, and protection against numerous predators. Always it will be in competition for those fundamental needs with its neighbours, and most seeds will be adequately provided in some respects. As a result most seeds will fall short of the perfect plant that we hoped we should see when we planted it. If we come across the plant half-grown we can help it along a little and make up for a few of those early deficiencies, but not all of them.

In a similar way we came into the world in circumstances that are common to mankind in that we had a mother and, probably, a family, but unique to ourselves in that nobody else had both our mother and father and our place in the family. These facts and these people have shaped us, genetically and environmentally, in ways which are partly obvious to us, like family rules about cleaning our teeth after breakfast and not before, and partly are buried rather deep. It is these deep-seated forces which concern us here. They are to do with the loves that we first experienced, sought, fell short of, the needs satisfied and unsatisfied, the rivalries we fought or refused to fight with our parents and our brothers and sisters, the resistances we met and how we were enabled to cope with them, the identities we looked for and found or lost, the illusions that we needed to shield us from too hurtful reality. We may as we begin to reflect on our childhoods feel the power of all those experiences and receive a hint of the uncomfortable fact that some of them may be with us still.

An example might be of help here. I had the excellent fortune to have been born into a secure, protective family (and we should understand that such a circumstance is simply good luck and we are in no way responsible for the family into which we happen to arrive). My father was for me a quiet, twinkling sort of man, a loving presence on the edge of the family, driven occasionally into decisive action by my strong mother, who was in her turn a caring person too, whose care I felt. I grew up, almost at the bottom of the pile, among five sisters and a brother. I was rather afraid of my mother, a little distant from my father and understandably somewhat overwhelmed by all those sisters. I was quiet, shy, diffident. I very rarely showed my feelings and neither of my parents, subsequent to babyhood, shared much physical affection with me. The two facts were not unconnected. What happened? I entered adulthood greatly confused about relationships with the opposite sex, since I had so many women about me but all, so to speak, of the wrong kind, and I had no skill in exchanging affection. When I met authority I would either be obedient or become sullen, reacting in the only way I knew to the strongest authority I had experienced, my mother. I fought battles with other authorities as if they were my mother without any idea of why I was behaving in that way, and I did not know why I felt so shut off from people. It took me many years to come to terms with all of that, to comprehend what was happening, to bring those hidden and painful feelings out of their hiding places and to begin with other people I loved to re-build my life in the shape that I felt right for me.

It will not have been the same for my brothers and sisters, who had a different place in the family, and neither may you have recognized just those experiences. No matter. What I am trying to explain is the enduring nature of these early experiences, the way that they still live with us in our adulthood. These are a large part of the strange forces we feel churning away inside us. And these are a major source of those judgments about good or bad emotions with which we are concerned.

In practice, then, there are several voices speaking to us about the emotion of jealousy all at the same time and it is not quite clear whether these voices are from outside or inside us and how we can decide. Our parents may still be alive and well and may, if we ask them, relate quite different experiences to the parents that still speak out of our interior. Parents are people too, they move on and grow and may have left far behind the voices that spoke to us when we were children and which still speak to us with that voice. The church too is a living and growing organism with its own contemporary voices but a portion of our early experiences in the church may now be speaking to us from inside us.

The authorities we seek come to us all jumbled up. We can, if we wish, choose an authority that suits us but we are unlikely to find common agreement anywhere about whether a particular emotion is good, bad or indifferent.

If then we cannot find a sensible answer to the question, who does in practice decide whether an emotion is good or bad? perhaps we could ask ourselves a similar question and see where that might lead. We could ask: Who should decide? Whose business is it to make such a judgment? Who or what is the bedrock upon which we may safely rest?

If everybody is, from an emotional point of view, like ourselves — and that is a premise from which this book begins — then we can now see that it would be folly to rest any final authority in any one being and even more in any group of them. We are all as frail as each other. We do without question discover ourselves in relationship to people. We cannot do without our neighbours for they are the seedbed of our growth. But their very fragility makes it impossible for us to place any ultimate reliance upon them as people, however much respect we may feel we owe to their office or to their personal qualities. Many people have said to us and will say to us, 'This is a bad emotion, this is a good one', and they may be right, but we have no grounds for trusting it on their own authority.

There must be a sense in which God is the bedrock of our morality. A creator cannot escape final responsibility for his creation. But who do we call God? The nearest I can get is the Father of our Lord Jesus Christ, yet millions worship a different God and do not share that belief. Millions too build their God in a shape that frightens me to death. I want nothing to do with a God like theirs. Just to say 'God' is to beg the question since we will then properly be required to give content to the God we worship, and we are immediately back where we started.

There is, however, one practical way in which God is always the bedrock and that is in the sense that he makes all else relative. Relativity is quite a worrying concept, and a complex one too. In the scientific world the only way I have ever been able to approach an understanding of it is by the example of the fly and the train. If a fly, the poser runs, is flying in the corridor of a train at 10 mph and the train is travelling at 60 mph in the same direction, how fast is the fly flying? There is obviously no definite answer to the question because the speed of the fly depends upon the position from which it is viewed, inside the train, outside the train, from another planet and so on. In a religious context too there are no definite answers if relativity reigns, except that God is by definition the final truth and therefore that nothing and nobody else can ever be. The relativity of all creation in this sense therefore is simply another way of putting that old christian doctrine, that everything and everybody stands under the judgment of God.

The presumption remains that it is we ourselves who have to decide. We are the people whose business it is to make a judgment about what is a good emotion and what a bad one, not in the sense that we are an ultimate authority for anybody else nor that we shall be certainly correct nor that our judgment is fixed for all time but simply in the sense that we are in the end totally responsible for deciding for ourselves or for choosing an authority we shall call our own.

We have now reached the rather awkward moment when I intend to set myself up as such an authority. Having railed at some length against external authorities, I am somewhat diffident about producing a set of suggestions which at the moment cover what I feel about the morality of the emotions. I am in danger of acting in a way I have myself deplored, because I can get to feel very protective of my suggestions and turn them quickly into rules. You then stick your toes in, as we have all so often done when faced with rules or rule-givers, and you and I arrive quickly at an adversarial position which is exactly the state which for so long has been destructive of our emotional lives!

So before I produce my suggestions I would like to spend a little time describing what I mean by rules. Rules are essential, in my view, under two conditions. They are necessary for all of us when we are young children because we are not at that stage aware of the environment we have been born into and therefore of its dangers, like wandering on to the mainline railway track. These are what I call 'danger rules'. Rules are also indispensable for the maintenance of the communities we join – families, countries, schools, voluntary groups. Every community has to balance the needs of its members as fairly as it can. That is the purpose of a whole range of rules which must be enforceable and subject to sanctions. I term these 'community rules'. The first set of rules we grow out of, the second we do not, though of course, as I have emphasized, many of us spend a lot of unnecessary energy fighting the second lot of battles in terms of those we should have grown out of.

All community rules are 'rules of thumb'. By this I mean that none of them is absolute. This follows from the fact that everything and everybody is relative except for God who maintains their relativity. This must apply to every single rule that has ever been made, even those that are as hallowed by tradition as the ten commandments. Even such a decisive rule as 'Thou shalt not kill' is in practice hedged with conditions. This is not to say that such rules may not be true, or certainly true enough for us to live by, but it is to say that we cannot be absolutely sure. We have to decide.

It is therefore true that every community rule – and as young people start growing up, more and more danger rules too – need to be in principle negotiable. They need to be able to be changed. This is not the same thing as saying that they should be changed, but rather to bear witness to their relativity. If we in our capacities as bearers of authority in homes, schools and other communities practised such negotiation more frequently, we should have more compliant charges in the present and more integrated adults in the future.

It is in that sort of spirit that I would like you now to consider my rules of thumb about 'good' and 'bad' emotions.

Firstly, then, I believe it to be true that all our emotions are in essence morally quite neutral. It is not correct to call an emotion in itself good or bad. To feel anger, jealousy, sexiness, hatred or pride does not have the automatic property of badness nor can we necessarily be called good because we feel loving, relaxed, happy, affectionate or kind. Perhaps you have already begun to sense that to be the case, as I have, in my attempt to make two opposing lists like that. Anger falls naturally into the 'bad' list but we have seen that we do not find anger always undeniably bad. There are occasions when it is positively refreshing. Kindness must be part of the 'good' list but, as Coleridge once said and as we all know,

> O worse than all! O pang all pangs above
> Is kindness counterfeiting absent love.

Each of the emotions, as we consider it more closely, seems suddenly to reveal a reverse side.

Or if it is not the reverse side, at least we find we have to take into account the context of the emotions. There are few who would frown upon sexiness in marriage, which these days causes few problems for the moralist. All the anxieties arise when sex, in spite of ourselves, spills over into the rest of our lives and we suddenly find ourselves feeling sexy when another part of us tells us that we should not. Or again it is quite a subtle exercise to distinguish between the natural and proper pride in achievements splendidly accomplished and the self-assured pride which cannot see itself as others see it. And why should we be judged virtuous because we feel happy at inheriting from an aunt? When, and for what reasons, emotions occur make a difference to how we judge them.

Moreover there are emotions which we cannot confidently fit into either camp. Sadness is no stranger to us. We may just be at a low ebb because our job is dull, our marriage not all that it should be and the children are raising hell, or we may be deeply hurt at the loss of a partner whose love has long been our joy and our support. Sadness has many levels of intensity. There are

few who would wish to make any moral judgment upon sadness
wherever it occurs. Sadness is neither good nor bad; it just exists.

Leaving on one side for the moment then that some emotions
without any doubt at all make us *feel* good or bad, I take as my
first axiom that nevertheless emotions in themselves are not to
be taken as either good or bad. They are no more moral or
immoral than hunger, warmth, touch or taste. All emotions are
morally neutral.

The second principle I would like to suggest is that we are not
responsible for the arrival of the emotions we experience in any
particular instance, though we may bear some responsibility for
patterns of emotions that emerge in our lives. Whatever the
source of our emotions – and we shall be examining that at
greater length in chapter 6 – we have no control over their
arrival. We suddenly discover that we are feeling envious or
warmly affectionate or monstrously angry and, even when we
know roughly what the feelings are about, there is nothing we
can do to prevent their coming.

I recall visiting one summer's day an ancient British encamp-
ment set up in a charmingly naive way to show us how our
rugged ancestors once lived. It was the actual site of the
settlement and situated in the midst of the huts was the original
spring which had led to their choosing the place those hundreds
of years ago. The cool water pushed its way up from beneath the
ground and ran quickly away. Nothing could stop it. It was alive
as it had always been alive. I gazed at it and reflected that if
somebody were to set a large block of concrete over the spring it
would prevent its arrival there yet would only ensure that it
erupted somewhere else. The spring was implacable in its
determination to be present to the world. In some such way do I
see the remorselessness of our emotions. They arrive, will not be
hindered and we are not accountable for their arrival.

I would expect this rule to generate rather more unease than
the last one. It is easier to see some rational sense in the view that
the emotions are morally indifferent than it is not to feel guilty
and blameworthy when our feelings appear to us to be bad and
pleased when they feel good. Many people, for example, who
are in general happily married feel ashamed because they are
attracted to somebody else whether it is a person of the opposite
or of their own sex. 'It's my fault,' they think to themselves, 'I
shouldn't feel like that'. Others are worried because of a flash of

anger they afterwards regret or a settled hatred for some mild-mannered neighbour who has done them no harm at all. Or some may feel delighted with themselves because they display an unheralded generosity or feel suddenly and unexpectedly loving towards somebody they have always previously found a pain in the neck. It is my view that they are on the contrary neither to be blamed nor praised for what they cannot help.

Of course, though I believe that to be a very important staging post in our understanding of the emotions, we cannot rest there. In practice we still feel good or bad in such circumstances and we still feel responsible for them. The natural man or woman wants to say, 'Come, come! We cannot let ourselves off the hook so easily. I know it isn't right to feel hatred for somebody. You yourself said in the last chapter that love of our neighbour is the new message of the kingdom of God. Hatred is bad and everybody knows it.'

So after concluding that the emotions are morally neutral and that we are not responsible for their arrival, the next thing to say is that we are totally responsible for what we do with them once they have arrived.

We need to distinguish carefully between that for which we are not and that for which we are responsible. There is nothing we can do about a chap stepping out of the shadows one evening in a dark street and threatening us, but what we do once he is there is entirely up to us (just as what he does is entirely up to him and our dual responsibilities may interact in a number of different ways). Our responsibility for our emotions rests not in the past, not behind us, not in the fact that they have arrived, but in the present, in the way that we take them in hand and act. This is the point at which the morality of our emotions comes into play, not a moment before.

We might, for example, be very afraid of our boss at work (and fear is another of those emotions which it is difficult to place on a moral scale). He glowers at us, speaks abruptly, doesn't let us know how he feels, demands very high standards. Our knees wobble and our stomach tightens when we go to see him. We are afraid of him, angry with him, angry with ourselves for not being able to cope with it all and driven into impotence. 'It's bad to feel so frightened', we think, 'I'm stuck because of it. I wish I wasn't so stupid.'

If we give it some thought, or somebody helps us to do so, we may come to see after a time that the fear we feel with our boss matches, it may be, what used to happen with our father. We used to be a bit afraid of him too, loving him but uncertain of his temper and keeping a wary distance. There is no need then to accuse ourselves of being 'stupid' because of our fear of our boss. Our fear has clear antecedents and is strictly 'not our fault'. Our present fear is a natural consequence of past conditions. But what we do now with that fear is our responsibility. Probably we need to lay down a few markers, to set up a few challenges, to test out the reality of our strength against his. However we act the onus for doing it rests upon us and nobody else. It may be true that 'my boss makes me feel frightened', but our fear is our responsibility, not his. He naturally has responsibilities of his own with respect to the fears that he engenders in others, but they are not to be confused with our own.

We need to go on to acknowledge that circumstances do alter cases. Some people have a whole lot more baggage from the past to carry round than others. This may make us more willing to sympathize and to offer help, less ready to be judgmental. It makes us understand how little responsible we all are for what has happened to us. It does not, however, take away one iota of those people's entire responsibility for handling their own lives, for taking or not taking the decisions that are necessary and acting on them.

Another circumstance that alters cases is the settled condition that arises out of an ingrained habit. If the boss has lived for many years by instilling fear into his subordinates and has thereby established a pattern of behaviour, we can appreciate that it is a great deal harder for him to change, because habit breeds inflexibility. It was for this reason that I said earlier that we may bear some responsibility for patterns of emotions that emerge in our lives. The fact that he instils fear will have its own antecedent explanations in the course of his life and for that he is not responsible. He has to take responsibility both for the fact that he has not earlier tackled the problem and thereby short-circuited the establishment of a pattern and for taking action in the present or for bearing the consequences of not taking action.

To say that we must always take responsibility for our emotions is not at all the same thing as saying that we shall always be in control of them. It would be foolish not to acknowledge that the expression of our emotions is sometimes irresistible and entirely

outside the control of our will. It is what we would expect
when we are handling the most explosive ingredient of human
existence. I recall talking to a man of a usually calm and equable
temperament who said that he had suddenly, and with utter
unexpectedness in the middle of the day, broken down into
uncontrollable sobs in his sitting-room. On reflection he knew
what the distress was about but he had had no inkling that he
had been so deeply disturbed and he was shocked at the
apparition of a self he had not known existed. We shall be
talking about the control of the emotions later (chapter 7). Here
we may simply need to see that, like unruly children, we are
always responsible for our emotions but cannot always master
them.

My rules of thumb then about the emotions are these:

– all emotions are in themselves morally neutral; they are
neither good nor bad

– we are not responsible for the emotions that arrive in us,
though we can affect their arrival by nurturing them

– immediately an emotion has arrived we are morally responsible for what we do with it

– sometimes an emotion overwhelms us; we do not thereby
become less responsible for it or for its consequences.

So what, you might ask, are the practical consequences of
approaching the emotions in this sort of way? How does all this
help? Let me spell out what I believe to be the main outcome a
little more clearly.

When we recognize that we are not responsible for the arrival
of our emotions, we begin to feel an easing of guilt.

I am not referring to those small pangs of guilt which are a
spur to action. Guilt in this sense is a conscious understanding
that there are things to be done and we have not done them or
actions we could have avoided if only we had been rather more
careful. When we are brought up short because we promised to
visit our elderly neighbour this week and it is now Saturday
evening and we have not been, that is a voice we should
pay attention to. A conscience which is carefully regulated
and monitored and attended to, without being permitted to
become a tyrant, can be a most healthy stimulant to sensible
achievement.

No, the guilt that I am talking about is that brutal, sour-faced old man of the sea who hangs around our shoulders and tries to drown us in depression. Perhaps it may be guilt for a settled feeling of anger which we cannot bring ourselves to express, an endless series of sexual imaginings we wrestle vainly to expunge from our minds or the intense jealousy that we feel about one of our spouse's friends.

It is not our fault that these sorts of feelings have arrived. Each of them has antecedents – a cause for the anger, the fact of sexuality, the difficulty of sharing love. Each of them might well be expected. If we can begin to admit to ourselves that we are not to blame for feeling as we do since we have absolutely no control over the arrival of such feelings, we might begin slowly to be freed from that sense of heavy guilt. Once rid of that burden, we become freer, more able to discuss what action it is that we should now take.

In sum, what I believe we should be trying to do, far from suppressing our emotions as we have often been taught, is to be learning to love our emotions as we love ourselves. For our emotions are the mainspring of our reality as human beings. To love our emotions is to love ourselves, and loving ourselves is, as we know, the condition of loving our neighbour, just as the forgiveness of our neighbours is the condition of ourselves being forgiven.

If all our emotions are morally neutral, it will do us no harm to love them, even though we might for a time feel them as bad.

4

Loving

You may recall that I spoke in chapter 2 of the kingdom of love that Jesus came to bring. He said that we were to 'love our neighbours as ourselves'. This was the description of the sort of love that God willed for us. Love meant that we were to look beyond all natural ties and antagonisms, to leap over all religious scruples, to set aside all hurts, imagined or real, and to accept as brother and sister whoever was immediately beside us. Nationalities and families were suddenly undermined, groups became dangerous, those who could expect little and constantly failed in their achievement of that little were nearest the kingdom, were most capable of displaying and accepting love. This was the 'new commandment', the astonishing revolution which even the church could neither fully comprehend nor dared to put into practice.

It is no easier today to find the courage to love like that. If we have not discovered a sufficiency of love shared among those from whom we could have rightly expected it, if we have not had the experience of the practice of love in our families, it is hard, sometimes impossible, for us to widen our affections. We cannot achieve what nobody has given us. Our capacity to love will only, to begin with, match whatever love we have received. Jesus did not expect the new kingdom of love to deny this love of the family, only to transcend it. Those who have been severely deprived of loving relationships in their young days cannot safely be introduced to the new commandment without first

working through, and coming to terms with, their early losses.
If they try to leap-frog that stage they inevitably practise a
phantom affection dangerous to themselves and puzzling to
receive.

Families teach us about loving, help us to come to terms with
our jealousies, make it possible for us to love two or three people
at the same time and in different ways, introduce us to the
concept of the group. Once this is achieved, our natural reaction
when we are out in the wider world is to recreate safe groups in
different forms, begetting substitutes for the family of origin
which in the course of time breaks up in any case and either dies
or makes new families. For this reason young people will form
gangs, and men and women, as well as marrying and building
families, will join clubs and churches, seeking out the like-
minded with whom they can feel 'a family' once more.

We also find satisfaction in knowing that we are part of
other natural communities. We know ourselves to be British or
American or Japanese, having distinct characteristics and taking
pride in them. Within those broad nationalities we have other
groups. I lived for many years in an English county which
positively revelled in its distinctiveness. It had the motto 'Du
different' and delighted to find ways in which Norfolk people
were original and inimitable. Or again we choose to join voca-
tional groups which give us a sense of being professional and
expert and from which all those not thus trained are excluded.

Jesus did not pretend that such groupings were unimportant
or suggest that they should be disbanded. He himself founded a
new group of like-minded men when he called out twelve
disciples for a special task, deliberately choosing to match the
number with that ancient group, the old tribes of Israel. There is
also evidence that even such a Jew as Jesus found his own
message about the widening of love's span hard to practise. A
Gentile woman once approached him that he should heal her
daughter (Matt. 15.21–28) and his first response was, 'I was only
sent to the lost sheep of the house of Israel.'

Groups then are inevitable and indispensable. What Jesus
claimed was that groups were not an end that we should seek to
achieve but a safe place out of which we should grow. The way
that he put it was that we should love our enemies (Matt.5.44).

The natural man wants to respond to that odd statement,
'Well, I haven't got any enemies', because we cannot often

identify in our hearts people towards whom we feel great
emnity. Even in wartime we recognize in our better moments
that 'the enemy' is largely a nationalistic cry for uniting a country
to achieve victory. 'Enemies' feels altogether too strong a word
until we begin to look more closely at how we feel about people
who do not fit in with our pre-conceptions. Sometimes it is two
or three 'problem' families, or black families, who move into a
road which has for generations been respectable and white.
Sometimes it is a bitter dispute in a local church over the type of
worship the church should use or the way a legacy should be
employed. Or it may be a Christian pacifist, actively opposed to
nuclear weapons, confronted by Christian members of the
armed forces committed to those weapons.

Abortionists, homosexuals, coloureds, layabouts, capitalists,
pagans, imperialists – as soon as we categorize people with
whom we disagree and do not permit them to exist as individuals
for us, as soon as we see people in groups and allow ourselves to
dress them up as caricatures, at that very moment they become
our enemies, opposed to us, not part of us, not members of the
group.

And that is the very moment that Jesus asks us to repudiate.
He does not deny any of the divisions that we struggle with, does
not ask people to cease being members of the group to which
they belong, does not ask us to change our opinions and agree
with whoever we happen to be alongside. He just bids us see
them as people and thus to break through into love.

What Jesus discovered in a very short ministry was that it was
those who had, and who could expect, very little who were most
receptive to his message. He began by hoping it might not be so.
He began in the synagogues of the land, appealing to those
honourable men who were steeped in Jewish law and practice.
They could not hear out of the closed groups to which they
belonged. It was left to women and children, to prostitutes and
quislings, to fishermen and zealots, to the sick and the poor who
had nothing to bring but their woes, to respond. These were
they who, one way or another, had been driven out of safe
groups or were, like women, too little considered to be seen as
groups at all.

I have felt it right to lay the rigour of the new commandment
before you at some length because the more we recognize its
seriousness the greater the distress it can cause at the very heart

of our emotional lives. The pressing question is this: Granted that the command to love our neighbours includes the love of our enemies, what happens if we do not in fact feel loving towards the neighbour or the enemy who is immediately beside us?

After all we meet a great number of people with whom we can barely be polite, let alone dredge up any love for them. To be asked to pretend to love them is a recipe for hypocrisy. We cannot be ordered to love somebody. Nobody can compel their feelings in one direction or another. Love is either there or it is not. A natural attraction or compassion may draw out the love in us, and if they do not we can at least remember our manners and do the best we can for them, but we cannot be expected to change our feelings. Yet if we do act lovingly towards people we can barely stand the sight of or to whom we are quite indifferent, are we not being classically hypocritical since we are openly sailing under false colours?

Such fears about the new commandment are widespread in the church and markedly inhibit the lives of many Christians. Believing that they ought to be in control of their emotions or despairing that they ever will be, they approach their fellows with a reserved wariness or a brash bonhomie which are instantly detectable and widely resented. The Christian outer face smiles and says, 'It's very good to see you', a Christian inner honesty protests on the contrary, 'Oh, not you again!' and conscience growls, 'Hypocrite!' Whenever we suppress the second honest voice the encounter will bear the certain mark of true hypocrisy, which is the act of deceiving ourselves.

I hope you may have recognized, having read so far, that the dilemma is a false one and arises out of a simple misunderstanding. It is true that emotions and feelings cannot be commanded. It is also true that a loving feeling is either in us or it is not. But if we remember that our feelings about this person are morally quite neutral and that we are not responsible for experiencing them, we can reflect on the person before us for whom we cannot feel any affection whatsoever and tell ourselves with complete frankness and no whit of shame, 'My feelings for this person are completely negative. I am not responsible for feeling like that and I do not need to blame myself. That is simply the way things are at the moment.'

What a blessed relief such recognition brings to us! All of a sudden our feelings are freed from condemnation. We are permitted to be honest, to feel affectionate towards that one and hostile to that one without being 'wrong' or 'bad'. We can say openly to ourselves (but not, naturally, to the person directly for reasons we shall see in a moment), 'You have a face like a ripe tomato and I can't stand the sight of it.'

There might well, later, be an extraordinarily valuable lesson to be learned out of our encounters. Although we are not responsible for the feelings that arise, we have seen in earlier chapters that all emotions have clear antecedents. They do not float in air. There may have been a direct but unrecognized memory. The person with a face like a ripe tomato reminds us unconsciously of a bucolic uncle who abused us, emotionally or physically, when we were small. That will take some honest but painful unravelling. It may be more complex than that. The authority with which another person confronts us, for example, might make us half aware of a decision we have been evading for some time or of a feeling of inferiority we could do well to identify more accurately. Similarly we might find that the person who bowls over our affections at first glance is inviting us to escape from a loving relationship closer to hand we have been neglecting, or is very like our favourite sister or brother. Whoever we meet and whatever we feel about them there may be work to be done afterwards.

We are aware of course that there is more to be said. Since we are responsible for what we do with our emotions and feelings once they have arrived, we must openly and honestly admit to ourselves that, whatever their antecedents, the feelings we have belong to us. It is not particularly pleasant to wish that the person before us would drop dead, especially if we live under the Christian command of love. We would all much prefer that our feelings were always cheerful and positive. But if we can bring ourselves to accept the negative feelings as belonging to us at least we have the contrary joy of taking the loving affections as our own too.

What we cannot say is, 'Because I cannot help feeling hostile to this person, as you say I cannot, therefore I will glower at him or turn my back on her.' The illogicality rests with the word 'therefore'. For we can choose what to do, or rather we can choose in any circumstances except when we are overpowered by emotions which are too strong for us. If we want to glower or to turn our backs there is nothing to stop us doing so, only we must take the responsibility for what we do and bear the consequences. If we choose on the contrary that our behaviour will not be governed by our feelings and we smile good-humouredly or at least listen attentively instead, then we are able to do so.

But, you will argue, does this not bring us right round in full circle to the position of the hypocrite who feels one way but acts another? By no means, and for this reason: that feelings and actions have no necessary connection nor is the one necessarily dependent on the other. Between what we feel and what we do lies the will, separating the two realities, not in essence subject to either. Christian love arises in the first instance out of our intention to care for people, whatever internally we feel about them. The Greek New Testament uses a special word for this, *agape*, and I call it the will to care.

One of the very best examples of the will to care arises in the story of the Good Samaritan (Luke 10.25–37). We must remember as we read it that it is the only story in which Jesus deliberately describes at any length an act of love and we should therefore be able to take it in many respects as definitive for the Christian.

The Samaritan then first responded to need calmly and efficiently. He did his best for the man who was hurt, disinfecting the wounds with wine and oil and binding them up. When he arrived at the inn, the story continues, 'he took care of him', altering his own plans for the night, and the next day offered his own money, committed the man to the inn keeper's care and said he would cover all further expenses as well. He gave therefore time, care and money, expecting nothing in return and making no attempt to bind the wounded man to him in the toils of gratitude. We are also of course aware of the hidden theme that runs through the story. Samaritans and Jews had been at loggerheads for centuries. Jesus chose to tell the story of a Samaritan caring for a Jew to make clear that it is God who chooses our neighbours for us and the Christian task is to love the enemy who is outside our own group.

There are two further points to make here about this sort of caring, the will to care, as I have called it, each of which, if not properly understood, undermines our ability to care by substituting feelings of guilt.

The first concerns our readiness to order our priorities or the extent to which we are subject to priorities apparently ordered for us by God. No doubt the Samaritan had many urgent duties of his own when he came upon the sick man. He deliberately interrupted those duties in face of the immediate call upon his compassion. It is impossible to overestimate that same message that comes to us directly from the practices of Jesus in his short missionary life. Charged as he was with the most crucial message for mankind, he yet allowed himself to be at times overwhelmed by the needs of those who came his way. It was his care for and healing of those who approached him, simply in response to a minimum of faith in himself and whether or not they became disciples, that was a part of the message that Jesus came to bring. He had to live the love of his Father for mankind as well as to preach it, and if the living of it sometimes swamped his ability to speak of it, so be it.

So for any Christian the priority of compassionate service cannot be in doubt. We do not practise it because it is a duty laid upon us by our faith but because it is an undistinguishable part of the faith itself. Not to care is an infallible sign that we do not have the faith of Jesus.

Nevertheless we have to ask ourselves what the Samaritan would have done, or ought to have done, if the robbers on the road from Jerusalem to Jericho had had a field day and there was not one wounded man lying by the side of the road but a dozen of them. He could not possibly have handled all that task himself. It may have been his duty, as in modern circumstances it may be ours, to have called in the contemporary equivalent, if there was one, of the ambulance service or to have alerted the authorities to a dangerous breakdown in law and order which they might have tackled at its root by rounding up the thieves and thus preventing any repetition of the outrage. But the call on his direct compassion would have been too great.

Modern Christians frequently find themselves in similar situations. There is just too much caring to be done. We do not know which of the appeals which drop through our letterbox at Christmas to respond to. We do not know which of the needy people about us most require our attention and if, through pressure of time, we are unable to look after somebody who asks for our benevolence, we feel guilty about it and often try to split ourselves in two, satisfying nobody. Soon, unless we are vigilant, the whole of our caring becomes burdened with the weight of those for whom we cannot care. In some circumstances it is not uncommon for the Christian's family to be the first to go to the wall. The summer picnic which the family has been promised for weeks is interrupted, shortly before departure, by a knock at the door which one of the family believes they must respond to, and the picnic does not take place. There is often serious resentment and disaffection lying unspoken at the heart of Christian families in which priorities always seem to lie elsewhere.

For it is priorities that are at issue. It is very unhealthy to be either at the giving or at the receiving end of guilt-ridden care. The feelings do not come out right. The carers feel martyred and the cared for triumphant. Reciprocal love, which is the only safe kind of love since there alone do we acknowledge that all love comes from God, becomes impossible.

We have to choose and to keep on making creative choices. We shall do this but not that, look after him but, as a consequence, be able to do very little for her. We have therefore to learn to say 'No' to pieces of Christian work which need to be done, and to people whom we should like to help. Any other way we are putting ourselves in the position of the omnipotent parent.

The second area in which guilt is at work in our caring is that of the giving of attention to people. If we have ever made a determined effort to listen to people talking about their troubles we will have reached a stage with some of them when our eyes become glazed and we think to ourselves, 'How much more of this can I stand?' Immediately we feel bad about that, dredge up a smile and try to resume our attentiveness, often without success. If we could only scrub their floor or cook their supper we should feel better about it, but they only want us to listen to them. Soon we are caught in a depressing spiral of alternate reluctance and resolution on our part and yet more demanding volubility on theirs.

One common reason for garrulity is not hard to trace. An astonishing number of adults do not really see children as people at all. Children are not treated seriously, are not listened to as if they might have anything important to contribute, are only heard as indulging in childish prattle. Certainly all children have a lot to learn. What adults so infrequently afford them is their unique contribution to the group as a whole. Some of those children brought up in this way therefore, needing to be recognized as individuals, may try to gain the attention of adults by talking more and more and being heard with increasing irritation. In adulthood they cannot escape the pattern of their childhood and keep talking, delighted when they have somebody listen to them but by now without any expectation of being understood.

This indifference to the person, which may live alongside some affection given in other ways, is what we, as listeners, are faced with and the cycle can only be broken by giving very serious attention to what the speaker says. It is often referred to as 'listening to the music of the words', which means that we need to train ourselves to hear the feelings that are being expressed by what is said. Often just the odd phrase will give us a clue about their unhappiness or resentment or excitement and we may have to learn to intervene, to help them pause and to speak, if they wish, out of the depths of their feelings, as they have rarely spoken before.

The trouble about it of course is two-fold. On the one hand they are not used to being properly heard, to being treated with a genuine seriousness and our attempts to help them pause will be rejected time and again. It is too painful, too unfamiliar, to be met as a person. On the other hand we may have had similar experiences of our own in our younger days and the reluctance to meet as authentic individuals may be ours as well. In either case there is work to be done. It will help neither of us to keep disabling each other with feelings of a shared guilt.

The will to care then is the mark of Christian loving and it can be achieved even if the practice does not at once, or ever, accord with what we feel. But that may sound a poor substitute for what we have always taken to be the fullness of Christian love. We do not want Christian love to arise simply out of our will. We both want and need to feel loving as well. What is the good, we might ask, of our will being converted to good works if our heart always lags behind and is not converted too? We are pressingly aware that in many respects our feelings are closer to our reality as a person than our will is and it is a cold fish who hands out charity because he is bound to do so. We want to hand out affection because we love to do so.

We must remind ourselves again at this point that we do not need to blame ourselves for not feeling loving. It is a fact, if rather a bleak one, that we are not able to share any more love than we have learnt. That does not mean that we are paralyzed for ever by the experiences we have undergone. We grow in two ways. Partly there are people who later in our lives offer us an unconditional love and we are surprised by joy, flowering under their care. Partly we have to learn, step by step, to take risks on our side, to offer our vulnerability and to discover that there are people who will not take advantage of it but will offer us theirs in return.

Love grows as we practise it. The grace of God moves in the hearts of those who are strictly honest about their feelings, who listen to their neighbours with a loving care, hearing the music of their words, who give attention to what they themselves feel, continuing to readjust the jigsaw picture of their lives. As we come to live with our shackles and reticences, as we live more comfortably and less judgmentally with our emotions, as we understand more about the reasons for the effect that certain people have upon us, the compassion that moved in the heart of the Samaritan moves in us too. But we cannot force ourselves to feel loving, cannot force the hand of God.

There is another kind of loving which keeps interrupting this comparatively peaceful scene of Christian love. Sexual love is no respecter of boundaries. Much as we should like, and even intend, to keep it safe within marriage it will not be confined. As we are innocently engaged in listening to a neighbour or fetching their books from the library we suddenly discover that we are beginning to feel attracted to him or her. We now see them as a sexual being and, however much we strive to keep this separate from our Christian loving, it will not go away. It is not exactly that we want to take them off to bed there and then or that we have fallen deeply in love, though occasionally we might, it is rather that there is a shift in our feelings towards them. We now feel them as potentially sexual whereas before we did not. The feeling is not irreversible in any particular instance. We may be enthralled one day and astounded that anybody so charmless could attract us the next. It seems to be a matter of moods, of chemistry as people say.

Now before we go any further we ought to give some attention to those who might say, 'Now, look. I don't know why you want to go on about sex in a book about the emotions. Sex isn't

an emotion at all. Sex is physical. It comes in the same sort
of bracket as hunger and thirst. It is a need that has to be
satisfied.'

There is certainly something to be said for this view. It is true,
strictly, that sex is not an emotion in the same sense as fear or
jealousy, for instance, are emotions. Sex is very clearly attached
to the physical and at its consummation always expresses itself
that way.

Yet two things need to be said about that. The first is that the
other emotions are not quite as non-physical as appears at first
sight. We shall see in a later chapter where I try to examine the
nature of emotion itself that when they are looked at more
closely the apparently 'internal', 'spiritual', call them what you
will, emotions have a surprisingly high physical element. For
example, fear might manifest itself in a cold sweat (which I have
had experience of knowing is not simply a euphemism), shaking,
changing colour, becoming frozen to the spot, muscular con-
tractions in the stomach, to name but a few possible symptoms.
Fear can often be relieved in a physical way too. The simple
removal of a frightening mask to reveal a neighbour's friendly
grin can rid us in a moment of physical symptoms and inner
fears together. We far too readily hypothesize about an outer
and an inner man and do not see the God-given unity of our
nature.

We also need to see that sex is by nature not something that we
do or possess on our own. Sex is only relevant in relationship to
somebody else. This is when it flowers. This is its focus. It is
therefore not precisely an equivalent to hunger and thirst which
are personal to the individual. When we are hungry we feed
ourselves. When we wish to express ourselves sexually we need,
if only in imagination, somebody else to share it.

And of course, as we all know, sex, whether expressed
physically or not, is for most of us at least some of the time as
close a relationship as we are ever likely to reach with another
human being. Sex explores, reveals and fulfils our love. It
cannot be detached from love.

We need therefore to talk about sex in Christian loving, and
we are all aware that it is often as worrying as it is fulfilling. In
the prime of life men and women instinctively seek partners,
and sexual feelings are then at their height. But they are not
confined there. Older men and women, whose married sexual

life perhaps has become ordinary, are excited by people twenty years younger or enchanting people of the same age. More worryingly, some of us may find that we are attracted by people of the same sex. We scarcely dare admit it, even to ourselves because we fear that we might then have to confess to homosexuality, perversion and a lot of other things that the Bible treats with some harshness. Most worrying of all, we may occasionally discover in ourselves sexual feelings in our dealings with children. A very young teenager grins at us out of the corner of their eye and makes us feel suddenly sexy, or we even hug our own junior school age child and feel an unexpected flirtatiousness arising between us.

Or it may be nothing quite so overt as that. It is not that we have particular sexual feelings towards certain people but rather that we find ourselves more generally sexual than we have always been taught it is right to be. Sexuality keeps intruding inopportunely. Part of the trouble is that many newspapers, magazines and modern novels place an emphasis upon sexuality which we cannot avoid noticing, even though we know that much of what they present is a barren, loveless sexuality which we are all better off without. But they are speaking to a part of us which responds positively or negatively to what we see and hear.

These sort of remarks will not make sense to every Christian. Some may be shocked that it can even be hinted at that sexuality is present anywhere except in marriage and may feel that it is better spoken of reticently even here. Others may never have been sexually aroused, for all kinds of different reasons, and therefore all talk of sex is bewildering, like visiting a foreign country. Yet others, warmly affectionate in their marriages, stand at the threshold of discovering their sexuality in all their relationships and are afraid of where it will lead them.

All of us, nevertheless, have to learn to live together in the church and to meet those outside. We all have relationships in which sex is a joy or a hazard. We need to find some common ground, some way to put sexual feelings into perspective. What ways are there of doing this?

The early church, as we have seen in chapter 2, approached sex exceedingly warily. It was anything from a distasteful necessity to an odious degradation, and it is this attitude that has prevailed in the church until relatively recent times. It is fair to say that the church historically has persecuted sexuality remorselessly and is still tempted along the same paths.

The church has battled for centuries, and in certain parts of it still battles, to maintain the celibacy of its ministers for no decent theological reason but because to engage upon a sexual relationship is seen as a lesser, a more worldly, a less spiritual calling than to be single. To quote the Book of Revelation again: 'Of all mankind they are the only ones who have been redeemed. They are the men who have kept themselves pure by not having sexual relations with women' (Rev. 14.3,4). Latching on to the so-called double standard, propped up by such stories as the rich young man to whom Jesus appeared to offer a softer and a harder path (see especially Matthew's version of the story, 19.16ff.), the church has applauded the higher reaches of spirituality, those attained only without money, will or sex, as preferable to the lower state of matrimony and worldly affairs.

There is no good biblical reason why the church should have done this. The Old Testament from the moment when God saw that it was not good for man to be alone (Gen.2.18) has numerous stories that delight in the love that a man shares with a woman. I do not recall a single passage that recommends celibacy (save for Jer.16.2, for whom it is presented as a heart-rending loss) nor would we expect it in a race that took such pride in their progeny and where women take such a prominent, if secondary, place in the life of the family. And at the heart of the Old Testament, between the psalms and the prophets, lies the magnificent love poem, the Song of Songs, which the church found so hard to take at its face value that even after seventeen hundred years they were stretching credulity to the limits by presenting it in the authorized version of the Bible as an allegory of the love of Christ for the church.

Jesus too was perfectly at home in the world of the emotions[1]. His relationship with women was without a practising sexuality because what he had to do could only be done alone, just as some people are still called to a single state in order to fulfil a particular task (or others suffer it because they have lost the one they loved). Yet he was free enough with women to cause grave scandal and he had special friends among them, like Mary Magdalen who in the garden of the resurrection was specifically asked by Jesus not to touch him for the obvious reason that she went to give him a hug as she had always done.

We have travelled far and in the right direction therefore from the Anglican prayer book of 1662 which spoke of marriage as a state designed to 'satisfy men's carnal lusts and appetites, like brute beasts that have no understanding' and for 'a remedy against sin, and to avoid fornication' to that of 1980 which says that marriage is given 'that with delight and tenderness they may know each other in love, and, through the joy of their bodily union, may strengthen the union of their hearts and lives'. We can no longer treat sex as anything but 'a gift of God in creation', a gracious offering from God whose purpose is as much to ease the exchange of love as it is to procreate children. The church must learn this lesson quickly. The world has had its way with sex for far too long.

If it is no longer possible then for the church to maintain the equation sex equals wrong or the erotic equals sin, what other ways can we discover for making sexuality not only creative but also safe? For we must be in no doubt that the sexual experience is very powerful and we need to find means of making it our instrument and not our master.

At this point especially I may be put under some pressure to produce a series of answers or inventions which will help us to deal once and for all with this business of sex. Surely, we think to ourselves, there must be some sort of heavy cudgel which will finally lay this bogey to rest. What can we do about all these feelings that rush so unexpectedly upon us? When I went to that evening class and my insides absolutely melted when I saw that man across the room and I recognized he was responding to me too, how can I cope with that short exchange of love and with the fact that I have back at home a husband who is loving, kind and affectionate, as I am with him? Sex is so thoroughly irresponsible.

A heavy cudgel is usually our first resource. We feel somehow it must be possible to bludgeon this feeling into insensibility. It is wrong to feel like this so we must kill the feeling. In that odd way we have of addressing ourselves internally, we deliver lectures to the sexual side of our nature and tell it to go about its business. Alas! it rarely does. And if we do apparently succeed what can happen is that we begin the destruction of all our sexual nature. We tell ourselves that sex is wrong and it becomes wrong therefore in our marriage too, and we wonder why things are not going too well with our spouse.

A bludgeon is a useless weapon against sex. There are some perfectly straightforward measures to take about the man (or woman) in the evening class. We can talk to him or her and begin to learn what sexuality is between two people who are perfectly sure that they do not wish to interfere with their respective marriages by any type of physical union with one another. We can talk to our spouse and share the pains of jealousy and the joys perhaps of taking a recrudescence of sexuality back into the marriage. If temptation is too strong and we doubt that our sexuality is yet mature enough to manage any closer meetings, we can quietly withdraw from the evening class.

My point is that the action we take is dependent first upon how we think about sexuality in general. My view is, as I keep making clear, that we are not one whit responsible for the feelings that arrive in us. There is absolutely nothing we can do about feeling attracted to this person but not to that one. We cannot help, and are not to be blamed or to feel blameworthy, for sexual feelings that arrive out of a cloudless sky.

Moreover, those feelings in themselves are not 'wrong'. They are not moral in any way. All emotions, as I have said, are morally neutral, neither good nor bad. We might feel them as good or bad but my view is that the Christian should view them just as we view good and bad people. Our first judgments about such people are often wildly inaccurate; the good we come to find self-righteous and the bad endearing. We just get it wrong, and we are much better employed witholding all judgment and, as we are bidden, 'loving our neighbours as ourselves'. In the same way we need to learn to love our sexual feelings as we love ourselves. For after all they are part of the selves we are bidden to love.

Once the feelings have arrived of course we are responsible for what we do with them. We do not, as I have repeatedly said, in most circumstances have to be governed by what we feel. We can choose whatever response we wish to make to the sexual situation that faces us, only remembering that, when we touch, there may in the long run come a point, different for different people at different times, when the forces become irresistible and our bodies take over.

But that is the difficulty. We cannot always accurately discern the limits of affection, often do not know our bodies well enough. Sexuality is so impertinent, and we are quickly the victims of our own conscience or our neighbour's harsh judgment or our family's suspicions of disloyalty. We understand only too well that it is as much a matter of motives as of actions. Suppose somebody hugs us or our children or our spouse. It might be marvellously releasing, feeding the growth of affection in all our lives; it could be perfectly acceptable if not especially helpful; we might find it a diabolical liberty which offends us and drives divisions between us and the intruder; or it might have the makings of a dangerous assault which we should resist with all the power at our command. Only we will know whether it does or does not 'feel O.K.', as we say.

If you wanted me to I could quite happily go on to make a general rule of thumb, as I have done before. If pushed then I would commend to you this: 'Do not abuse anybody for any reason.' I don't suppose anybody would dissent from that and it is surprisingly comprehensive in the field of sexuality once we start thinking about it.

But frankly I do not believe such rules are of much value in the rough and tumble of everyday life when we are faced with excitable involvements and hurried decisions, and we cannot quite see whether we are taking a calculated risk or falling over a precipice. Christianity has never taught mature Christians to live by rules, however admirable. We have to submit ourselves to the lively Spirit of Christ, and by and by we take some kind of step which may or may not turn out to have been desirable.

We learn by experience, claim forgiveness if necessary and proceed quietly upon our way, guided perhaps by the amiable story of the company of porcupines. Finding themselves very cold one winter's day they huddled together to profit by one another's warmth and to avoid being frozen to death. However, they immediately felt the sharpness of one another's quills and drew apart again, only to discover that they were cold once more. So they were driven backwards and forwards between the desire for warmth and the fear of sharpness until they found a tolerable mean where they were not too much hurt and sufficiently warm.

5

Being Angry

Tamar was a very beautiful girl. The sister of Absalom, King David's son, and not betrothed to anybody, she came to the notice of Amnon, Absalom's half-brother, who fell in love with her. In fact he became totally obsessed with her and plotted to have his way.

He pretended that he was ill and asked if Tamar could come and wait on him in his sickness. Soon after she arrived he turned everybody out and asked Tamar to come to bed with him. She indignantly refused. 'It would be disgraceful for both of us,' she said, 'and anyway I'm sure the king would consent to our marriage if you asked.' Amnon raped her nevertheless and then, because she would not go voluntarily, had her thrown out (II Sam 13).

The result of this sorry tale was a number of angry people. Amnon, with a terrible lack of justification, shook with passion against the wronged Tamar. 'Get this woman out of my sight!' he bawled at the servant. Absalom, who took Tamar in, was so angry with Amnon that he held a feast two years later, invited Amnon and had him killed then. King David was furious, but not so furious that Absalom, after causing Amnon's death, feared for his life at David's hands and fled. Of Tamar it is simply recorded that she was 'sad and lonely'.

Much earlier (Gen. 4.1–9) we are told that Cain, too, 'became furious, scowled in anger' and struck down his brother because, for reasons we are not told, 'the Lord was pleased with Abel and his offering but he rejected Cain and his offering.' Here the anger seems to have arisen out of a sense of injustice. It wasn't fair.

The two stories illustrate for us some of the springs of anger. At the centre of it all is a conviction that the participants have been wronged, whether it is an individual like Cain, or another who is cared for, like Tamar. We feel the repressed anger in Tamar who takes her anger back into herself and becomes withdrawn. We share the fury of Absalom and David in recognition of the barbarity of Amnon's crime. We feel distressed for Abel because he becomes the innocent victim of Cain's anger; it was no fault of his that the Lord had accepted his offering and not Cain's.

A sense of injustice, of having been hurt, lies at the heart of all our anger. Hurt directly, hurt by being misunderstood, hurt by neglect, hurt on behalf of those we love. It is one of the hardest of the emotions to handle either in ourselves or where we meet it in others. We may be a little aware of what I shall refer to later as 'anger's freeing power' but most of us are much more used to the way that it can lock us in. We can be locked in not only by the anger of others that freezes our soul; we can equally well be locked in by a habit of our own precipitate anger which keeps destroying the welling love in us.

It fights so brazenly with our longing to be people of love. We have been taught from childhood, even in the majority of families who have but little connection with a religious faith, that we should be 'nice to people'. I have myself throughout this book expressed my conviction that the love of our neighbour as taught by Jesus is a revolutionary message, written indelibly upon the Body of Christ, which does not mean simply that we are required to display a bland affability to the world at large nor even that we are 'to do the best for everybody' but that we are charged with confronting our deep-seated hostilities and working to make love grow there.

Anger in practice seems too often to be the enemy of this love that we are all seeking; should we not suppress it? Yet, we go on to reflect, such suppression does not make anger disappear, only turns it into sourness or mock affection each of which is as effective a spoiler of the spirit of Christ as any display of temper. So we arrive back where we started, driven into confusion, making shift with a spurious distinction between righteous anger, which we can scarcely believe any but Jesus was righteous enough to display, and illicit anger which is all the rest of it.

So what are we to do with our anger? Must it always be a spoiler of the love of God and mankind? Must we be for ever hurt, for ever locked in? These are the sort of cries that sometimes reach us, especially if we are caught in a long-running private battle when anger and the fear of anger is the substance of the relationship.

I must answer right away that if we always see anger in terms of the harm it does then it will always do us harm. But if we are prepared to shift our vision a little and give attention to a side of anger we may not have seen before, it may still sometimes do us harm but we may also find it to be one of the most valuable spurs we have to the restoration of our brotherhood before God. It can be of inestimable value to the renewal of human loving.

I do not apologize for beginning again where I have started so frequently before by saying that, except in so far as we have allowed a settled habit to be ingrained in us, it is not our fault that we are angry. We are not responsible for the arrival in us of a feeling of anger. We probably will be blamed for being angry, but without justification, and we must not allow any external blame to be turned into a personal sense of blameworthiness.

Emotions just arrive. They have all sorts of antecedents, some of which if we look carefully we shall be able to descry fairly easily and many of which will be buried rather deep. There are reasons why we are angry and these reasons lie outside us. The presence of anger in us then has simply to be accepted as a fact without any attempt to sit in judgment upon it.

We must remind ourselves too that anger is not in itself wrong. Nothing of ours can be wrong for which we are not responsible, and we are not responsible for the arrival of anger. It is of the greatest importance that we should make this fact clear to ourselves because, if we do not, the very judgments we keep making against ourselves imperil the journey towards new life.

As always, we must go on to observe that, once anger has taken up residence in us, what we do with it lies in our hands. From time to time, of course, anger might overwhelm us. We might scream at the children in paroxysms of fury when they needle us right over the edge of our point of tolerance. There we are! That happens to everybody and we can just thank God that we are Christians who know that there is nothing unforgivable in all the earth, seek reconciliation and go serenely on our way. Customarily, though, we have our anger reasonably in hand and we are able therefore to recognize our responsibility for taking action. So what do we do?

The way I would like to proceed at this point is as follows. I first want to give you two workaday stories in which anger is a main ingredient. These I hope will help us to focus our minds on specifics.

I shall then go on to demonstrate a couple of devices we use to try and evade the issues of anger. Anger is wounding and we like to avoid being or causing hurt if we can. My view is that the followers of Jesus should never be surprised that the way to new life is through the cross, and I believe we need to confront the hurts and work our way through them. However, we all do attempt evasion and the evasions I shall be describing are first denial, in which we blithely say that we are not angry at all when everybody else knows we are, and secondly projection, when we are so unready to accept that we are angry that we pretend the anger belongs to somebody else.

After a look at an incident in the life of Jesus in which he displays his anger I finish the chapter by suggesting three steps on the road to coping with our anger:

– acknowledging that it is true;

– trying to discover why we are angry and in particular who we are angry with;

– putting our anger, once discovered, where it belongs.

I shall end by talking of the differences between destructive and freeing anger.

In the first of my stories, then, we have been quite ill for five or six weeks, unable to go out much and certainly not fit to go to church. The church members have not displayed much interest in our absence. One particular friend has been very good but nobody else has been round to see us and our rising anger finds a special focus in the minister who has not even enquired how we are, let alone made a visit.

On the face of it we appear to have two choices of behaviour. We say to ourselves or to our best friend, 'Oh, let's forget it,' or we can say, 'I'm going to go and have it out with him.' Neither way, to be honest, seems specially satisfactory. In the first case we are not ever going to see the minister in quite the same way again. We determine to forgive him and forget the whole business and we do our best. But we shall never quite trust him again, there are areas of discussion between us which will be for ever closed and a slight feeling of disappointment creeps into our Christian lives ('can I ever trust anybody again and, if I can't, what sort of a God is it that I worship?').

The other alternative of confronting him with our displeasure does not appear a great deal more fruitful. We don't quite know how he is going to take it. The best we can hope for is that he will say he is sorry and make his excuses, and we shall feel justified though perhaps a little self-righteous. But it might turn into a horrendous row. He may be very hurt and we will feel dreadful at adding to his burdens, or he may even turn on us and accuse us of the deficiencies we have displayed in our Christian life. We do not want to risk that sort of disruption in our lives or in the life of the church nor do we feel it right that we should be the direct cause of so much hurt. 'Let it lie,' we tell ourselves.

Defecting ministers are on the whole a part of a fairly distant world. They come and go, and the next one may suit us better. We cannot escape so easily from the situation in my second example which concerns a partner in whose company the wife often feels uneasily incompetent. There is a great deal of love between them, nobody denies this for a moment, but she so often feels inadequate. He doesn't say, 'Oh for God's sake, woman, why don't you say something sensible for a change?', though that would often be preferable because such an open challenge she could confront. Instead he works by way of hints and silent messages. When she has left the washing-up he will walk over to the sink with heavy steps and run the tap rather fast as she scurries to pick up the tea-towel. A bright, significant smile accompanies his 'Well done!' when she does or says something of which he approves. A sharp look is often enough to put her in her place and most times he doesn't even seem to be aware of his assumption of a natural superiority.

She is left to fume and smoulder in silence. She sinks into a settled anger which infects her relationship with everybody she meets and which there seems no means of dissipating. She lets her hair down to one of her friends occasionally and receives some comfort and, since this kind of suppressed anger so often expresses itself in fits of depression, may pay a visit to the doctor who will give her some mild anti-depressants. But still she remains speechless with rage when he deliberately moves the soap back where it belongs.

These sort of examples show us that one of the worst results of anger is the impotence that it induces in us. We are caught between expressing our anger and thus inflicting damage on the smaller or larger communities which are the source of all meaning in our lives, or bearing the anger inside ourselves, injuring our very soul. We have to find some ways out of this dilemma and two of the most common ones are denial and projection which I shall now go on to discuss.

Before I do so we need to note that, although I shall be talking about the denial and projection of one particular emotion, any emotion can be dealt with in these ways. Anger is only one of the emotions that cause us such ferment and all of them have to be dissipated in one way or another if we are not to collapse under their weight. There is not room in a general book on the emotions, such as this, to explain in detail how the processes work in the cases of jealousy, guilt, anxiety, fear and so on, but it will not take much of an imaginative leap to see how the same sort of things happen with them as well.

Denial is the simple refusal to admit that anger is present. It protects against the hurt of anger by pretending that it isn't there. It happens at the most elementary level in many areas of our lives, like the lady I heard of recently who worked in a large office and was responsible for making appointments and recording them in a book. As sometimes happens with all of us she muddled up two appointments and people turned up at the wrong time. When this was pointed out to her she denied it altogether. In spite of the fact that the names were written in her own handwriting she declared stoutly, 'No, it couldn't have been my mistake because I don't use that colour ink.' We find the most unlikely reasons for refusing to admit obvious facts which cast a reflection upon us which for the moment we are unable to bear.

In the same way we may deny our anger altogether. 'No, I'm not in the least angry,' either the church member or the wife may say protectively, frowning ferociously. Believing that anger is wrong or that it shows us up in a bad light we refuse to acknowledge its presence. The origins of such blatant lying are not hard to find. When we were young and flew into a rage, storming upstairs and slamming the bedroom door, one of our parents shortly followed us up and, provided we had not barricaded the door, shouted at us, 'Don't you dare be angry with me!' The unspoken message was that anger was impermissible or at least should not be openly expressed. Since we needed to retain our parents' love and we had now been given the clearest message that love was endangered if we showed ourselves to be angry an obvious way to resolve the difficulty was to pretend that we were not angry in the first place. Such old habits die hard.

We may, however, for the same sort of reasons, confess to ourselves that we are angry, or that we are probably angry, but determine that we shall not admit it especially to the person who is its immediate cause. 'It wouldn't do any good to say what I feel', we say to ourselves and sometimes that may be a fair assessment of how things are between us. More often it is pure funk and produces what I call the minefield effect in which we live with an area between us which it is dangerous to approach because there lie hidden potentially explosive subjects.

For example, the minister of a church, usually a mild man, but of whom many are a bit afraid, has put his foot down. That church organization will have to close down since it is no longer fulfilling its purpose. The members, few in number, are angry but it's a friendly church and they don't want to upset the good fellowship. So they say nothing. They nod and smile at the minister as they leave church on Sundays and he is pleased that they have taken his decision so well, and then they go and express their fury to other members of the church. Over the months the minister begins to worry because there seems to be some sort of constraint between him and them and they do not come and talk to him anymore. The anger has gone underground. It is not denied except where it matters most, to the person who is the cause of it.

This sort of selective denial in which all the participants live a lie is one of the most damaging factors I know of in the lives of families and groups the world over, producing at times communities of the most frightening impotence, sterility and illusion.

A third form of denial is more subtle. It is when we justify and therefore expunge our anger by comparing it favourably with that of our adversary. In the example I have already given, for instance, where the wife fumes at being subservient to her husband it is obvious to any onlooker that we have two angry people both of whom are denying their anger.

One day the wife explodes with anger to which her husband responds with an icy politeness. She, however, has been brought up to believe that anger is wrong, indeed her very suppression of it is evidence that she cannot openly allow such an emotion. Plainly to admit her anger even to herself therefore will put her in the wrong again and make yet more room for her husband's disapproval, disapproval which she has some instinct is itself a covert form of anger. She does not therefore deny her anger but says, 'His behaviour is quite disgraceful.' She has redirected her anger towards her husband's hidden emotions. She is now angry at his anger and proves thereby that she does not approve of anger. Thus her own anger is denied. Parents naturally do exactly the same with their children, claiming that what they call their severity is for their children's own good and giving themselves freedom to be as savage as they wish.

Here we are beginning to pass over into the second major way of managing our anger, that of projection, in which we discover in ourselves emotions which it is too stressful for us to carry so we make somebody else carry them for us. The emotion is too strong to be denied altogether and too hurtful to admit as our own. It must therefore belong elsewhere and we externalize it in the most appropriate person to hand.

It is most easily seen in a familiar device which all began in the Old Testament. There was an ancient Israelite ceremony in which an actual goat was seen as bearing away the people's sins.

> Aaron shall put both his hands on the goat's head and confess over it all the evils, sins, and rebellions of the people of Israel, and so transfer them to the goat's head. Then the goat is to be driven off into the desert by a man appointed to do it. The goat will carry all their sins away with him into some uninhabited land. (Lev. 16.21,22).

It is not difficult to appreciate the marvellous relief afforded by this simple ceremony. The desert was already seen as a place inhabited by demons and evil spirits hostile to mankind so it was fitting that all the people's burdens of guilt and failure should be carried away by the goat to join their associates in the wilderness.

Any individual or group can use the same manoeuvre to

displace pressure it cannot bear. It is often seen in families as in this example from a psychotherapist's casebook:

> The mother ... presented as a hard-faced, angry witch-like figure who blamed and scolded Susan (her 14-year-old daughter) while the child sat silent and sullenly depressed. As she heaped abuse on Susan, who was clearly being used as a scapegoat figure, the mother violently rejected any suggestion on my part, however mild or carefully phrased, that she might be partly responsible for a continuation of the child's resistance; instead she shouted, interrupted me, refused to listen when I asked her to do so, kept getting up and threatening to leave and then sitting down again.[1]

The psychotherapist, rather unusually, decided that he would have to meet her on her own terms and, shouting louder than she did, he roundly rebuked her for her behaviour which was quite as bad as her daughter's. He ordered her off the premises unless she was prepared to treat him with proper respect and she stalked off in a fury. This drastic shock treatment had the effect of assisting the mother to take back into herself some of the blame and guilt she had been heaping upon Susan. She understood that she had been making her daughter responsible for bad feelings which in truth resided in herself and, once she was induced to take back those feelings, she made it possible for Susan to have a balanced relationship with her again.

Projection does not always happen in such an obvious way. We all need to unburden ourselves of our guilt, to escape from images of ourselves which show us in a bad light, to create some kind of equilibrium within us. Simply to confess our sins in church or to God through an individual does not always relieve our deeper-seated anxieties. Indeed such confession can at times reinforce rather than assuage our guilt. So we resort to placing in other people, or occasionally in other things, the feelings in us which we take to be bad.

For example, I had a visit from a lady whom I shall call Sally, who had had an upsetting interview with a close friend of hers. The friend, who was living apart from her husband and had had a somewhat distant relationship with him matching the distance of her parents, had accused Sally of not daring to get close to her. She felt isolated and rejected, she had told Sally, and why could not Sally make a warm, loving relationship with her? Sally protested that she did love her but came to me anxious that she was in some way failing her friend. I suggested that much of that failure to love might as easily be in her friend as in herself. We looked at the way her friend had always kept people at a distance because she herself had been distanced by her family of origin. This would have been painful to experience and to accept and it would be more comfortable to accuse others of not getting close enough than it would be to admit that she herself was inherently distant. Hence the accusation of a failure to love was in part a projection of her own inability to love.

Only in part though, for we unfailingly find the people who match our inner conditions and our projections always come to rest in people or in objects which in some respects mirror ourselves. Sally was only beginning to come to terms with a background in which she had experienced little closeness. She too had felt isolated from her parents though she now was fast learning what had been left behind by that experience and was beginning to allow herself to be warm. So she was precisely in that position where her friend wished to be – moving away from the solitariness within her – and that her friend should, through an angry argument, project her impotence upon somebody in Sally's condition was inevitable.

We also have to learn that the projection was probably necessary. It is not a matter of blaming somebody because they are relieving the pressure upon their feelings. Sally's friend could not bear the tension between the warmth that somebody was showing her and her inability, through past deprivation, to respond to that warmth. She needed to project her helplessness to give herself time to grow.

Being on the receiving end of such projections is not comfortable. We find a vague and confusing unease, a sense of injustice or of guilt depending upon whether we choose to project the feeling elsewhere in our turn or to take the projection into ourselves. In either case we feel angry, sensing that our feelings are being manipulated and that the whole transaction is nothing to do with us at all. We need therefore to be able to identify projections. We have quite enough feelings of our own to manage without carrying other people's as well.

One sure way of recognizing projections is to give a closer and more dispassionate attention to our feelings than we ordinarily do. If we discover that what somebody tells us about our feelings does not conform to what we actually feel, if there is some kind of imbalance between that of which we are accused and what we know ourselves to be, then it is likely that the feeling does not belong to us. It is a projection. Sally did not feel herself to be, and was not, the loveless person which her friend said she was. Nevertheless in such cases, once recognized, we may have to bear the projection for the time until we can gently (or not so gently, as the psychotherapist decided!) return the feeling to the person to whom it belongs.

Denial and projection then are two familiar ways of managing all our feelings, and particularly our anger. But even if we manage to surmount these obstacles we are still left with the original dilemma. To hold on to our anger is injurious to ourselves, to express it is damaging to others. At which point it may be helpful to examine an incident in the life of Jesus, one of the many places in the New Testament where he is shown to have had strong feelings.

He was in one of the Galilean synagogues one sabbath day early on in his ministry and they were all watching him closely to see if he would heal a man there who had a withered arm (Mark 3.1–6) for already his reputation as a sabbath-breaker was gaining ground. He took them on, had the man out in the middle and challenged them, 'Is it lawful to do good on the sabbath day? Or to do evil? To save life? Or to destroy it?' Nobody said a word. 'And he looked round at them angrily', the account continues, 'inwardly very upset because of their hard hearts.' He healed the man and the Pharisees immediately left to lay plots with the Herodians against Jesus' life.

There are several interesting points about this story. The first is that here, as elsewhere in the Gospels, Jesus had no inhibitions about expressing his anger. He openly displayed what he felt. 'He looked round at them.' He found it very hard to accept that there were people who had their priorities so upside down that they thought it was more important to keep a legal ruling than it was to care for human beings. His sense of justice was outraged, which as we have noted is one of the mainsprings of anger. Yet he did not waste his time on his anger. He did not make it the focus of his complaint. His anger was an adjunct to their hard-heartedness and what was really at issue was that they did not allow themselves to care.

We may share those feelings. It is not only Jesus who can

appreciate that their priorities were crazy. We too are rightly angry when people do not come before rules. So this story, as others in the Gospels (Mark 8.32,33; Matt. 23; Mark 10.14), is permissive towards the expression of our anger and we do not have to separate off Jesus' anger into a separate compartment from ours as if his was 'righteous anger' and ours could never be.

At the same time we need to note that Jesus' anger was a response to the issue of his hearers' unsympathetic behaviour and was not the issue itself. It is all too easy for a person to hold emotional sway over an encounter, using anger to gain ascendancy irrespective of what he or she might be angry about. Jesus' anger was a human response to intolerable conduct. It was the behaviour and not his response that was fundamental.

The account uses a further word that illuminates Jesus' emotional responses. I have translated the word Mark employs 'inwardly very upset'. Jesus freely expressed his anger but there was a sadness in him, a distress, that tempered his wrath. He felt for the people involved. He was like the parent who sees his nearly adult child making an ass of himself and cries out silently in his heart, 'Oh, child! How could you be so stupid!'

And it is indeed this inner battle between our love and our anger which so often prevents us saying what we feel. We most frequently become angry with those we love most and to express our anger, we feel, may put that love at risk. The longer that anger builds up, like water behind a dam, the more frightening it feels, and sometimes a settled anger can have decades of experience behind it. At times we do not even dare to acknowledge that it is anger that we feel because the object of our anger is also the source, sometimes the major source, of our being loved.

Very many adults are choked with fury towards a parent, most frequently their mother, who has over the years done no more than to do their best for their child and who is painfully aware of their inadequacies. Not willing to hurt each other, the anger lies dormant, or more frequently is taken out on a confused spouse, and relationships everywhere are injured. It is often surprising how quickly such long-standing estrangements can begin to be repaired if one or another party dares to broach the subject directly. I am constantly amazed how frequently the deepest hurts require for their healing no more than that which is available to all of us, courage.

Jesus' courage was unquestioned, and its immediate result in this case was that his opponents had to face their own anger too. In fact St Luke's account of this same incident (Luke 6.6–11) draws attention to the Pharisees' anger (it is interesting how Luke often plays down Jesus' emotional responses and does not here make any reference to Jesus' feelings while Matthew, 12. 9–14, as always, excises every single reference to Jesus' inner life). They were filled with 'a sort of madness', Luke says, and put their heads together to try and decide what action they could take against Jesus. They thus displayed the classic response to an open expression of anger; they declined to confront it but gossiped among themselves, hatching plots, cursing Jesus, feeding their anger among those they could rely upon to share their feelings.

How easily we can recognize the behaviour of groups the world over, not least in the church, and how destructive such conduct is of a lively fellowship!

The incident shows us, then, that in Jesus' view the expression of anger is not wrong, indeed that the failure to express it can make mutual understanding impossible, but that anger needs to spring not simply from a sense of personal outrage but also out of a serious concern for those involved. Anger often properly belongs to a situation and is not a personal and malign intrusion into it. Its expression may upset the conventional Christian view that Christian communities should also be places of sweetness and light, yet an attack upon the community as it presently exists may be the only way that its integrity can be maintained.

The Jews had become stuck in their conviction that nothing at all should be allowed to interfere with the maintenance of the sabbath. Jesus needed to demonstrate that this view was wrong and that care for people transcended the rule of law. It was anger that instantly clarified the issue.

This incident helps us to begin to see what a positive sort of emotion anger can be. It is an exploder of fantasies, a harbinger of truth, a discloser of reality. It can also on the contrary be the means by which the strong maintain hegemony over the weak, and an inhibitor of any growth in a community or an individual. So we need to look finally at the sort of process we need to go through if we are to be able to asess what sort of anger in any given instance we have to deal with and to wrest it to our advantage.

When we find then that we are angry the first step we need to take is to acknowledge that it is true. It seems an embarrassingly obvious course to commend, yet experience shows that, so frightened are we of anger, so certain that it will destroy, so convinced by years of teaching that it is sinful, that we will do practically anything to avoid looking at it. I have already described the processes of denial and projection. When our stomach is tight, our eyes flashing and our lips set we say sharply in blithe contradiction of facts which are obvious to the on-looker, 'I'm not in the least angry, as a matter of fact.' It is wrong to be angry, we cannot admit that we are angry, therefore we are not angry.

When we are unable to deny that there is anger in the air, to avoid having part in it we say or imply, 'It's not me who's angry.' Somebody else has to carry the anger which we will not acknowledge. If we are driven in the end to admit that it is we who are angry we become guilty, crying, 'God, be merciful to me, a sinner.' All this is most unhelpful.

Nor is it very profitable to practise a more subtle projection which is open to many Christians. Both Old and New Testaments speak of the devil or Satan, a principle or principal of evil active in the world working to overthrow God's handiwork. 'The devil finds work for idle hands to do', is the ancient cry while others believe that the devil takes up residence in people and they work to cast him out. We do not need to enter into the controversy over the form of the existence of evil in the world to appreciate that the devil can be a useful device for those who do not wish to acknowledge that they are angry. 'The devil's at work in me again,' they will say, as if the anger is an alien squatter who does not rightfully belong to the body he inhabits.

Although the subject may feel guilty at giving room to such a lodger he also manages to retain his own purity, for at bottom, he argues silently, the anger is not part of his real nature.

In contrast to all such evasions we need to assert that anger belongs to the person who feels it. We need to say, 'Yes I am angry. The anger is mine and not anybody else's. I am not a person in whom an anger foreign to me has taken up temporary residence. I am an angry person.' Only when we join ourselves to our anger can we take the emotion in hand and see what we need to do with it.

The next step is to make some attempt at elucidation. We

need to try and discover why we are angry. Of course at times it seems perfectly obvious. When the idiot drives into the back of our stationary car we leap out in a fury and tell the errant driver exactly what we think of him or her. Yet, curiously, the next time it happens we may treat it all very calmly and settle amicably for the exchange of a ten pound note. Why do we act so very differently in very similar circumstances?

It has to do with our own inner disposition at the time and the effect that the event has upon that dispositon. If, for instance, when our car is hit, we have been brooding for some time over a hurt inflicted by our spouse which we have not yet dared to bring out into the open, our anger at the other driver may be a deflected anger. We leap at the chance to rid ourselves of a pent-up emotion and the unfortunate driver receives a torrent of abuse quite out of proportion to his or her offence and not much to do with the event anyway. Or, more difficult to detect, the driver may, by the attitude he or she takes up, unconsciously revive memories in us of similar deep-seated interactions from the past. Perhaps it is a man who is effusively apologetic and we are silently reminded of the younger brother we once bullied unmercifully and whom now, in the shape of the sinful driver, we tyrannize again. So a quarrel over a bent bumper becomes a script re-enacted from our past, recent or ancient.

This sort of illustration gives us a clue to the most important question we need to ask to elucidate our anger: Who am I angry with? It may be the person who is the immediate cause of our anger or it may be another of our erstwhile or present companions. We have to decide. To which you might understandably reply, 'That's all very well. But in the first place emotions are by definition things that are felt and not things that are thought about. And secondly, even if we could think about them, there certainly is no time between the act and its commission to allow us to do it. When I'm angry I blow my top and that's it!'

These are serious objections which need to be attended to. The first says that thinking about our emotions is inherently impossible or logically contradictory. In practice I need to assert that it is not so. In fact 'practice' is exactly the word we need, for it is practice that begins to make it possible to think about our emotions. It is part of that self-reflectiveness which I have talked about in previous chapters as being one of the distinctive marks of the human being.

It is very hard work. It means that we have to pause and say to ourselves, for example, 'Now what exactly am I feeling? ... Yes, it is anger that I feel and not disguised jealousy or grief. Who am I angry with? ... Ah, it's my wretched teenage daughter who is getting up my nose again. She knows just how to bait me and I rise every time. Is that all I feel about my daughter? ... No, she's the apple of my eye and I adore her. Adore? Well ... A goddess then since only they are rightly adored? No, but ... Well, perhaps yes, a little. I'm uneasy there. Do I adore anybody else? My wife ... I used to adore my mother. I wonder if they liked it, if they like it. Do I then think that I am less important than they are, they goddesses and me a worshipper? Hm! Am I angry because women make me feel small?'

That is a perfectly possible train of thought over one's feelings about one's daughter. It is not clear at this stage of course whether it is fact or fantasy or how much of each is involved. We are somewhere along that bridge between the two and it is not too firmly rooted at either end (at the feeling end we do not know whether we are angry or loving and at the fact end we do not know how the women perceive us). And it is now therefore that it becomes possible for us to test out what we have been thinking and feeling, just as Jane Eyre did. We make some gentle approaches to our daughter, wife, mother, 'This is how I have been feeling. What does it feel like to you?' In return we may receive veiled hints, enough for us to work on, or strong positive or negative feelings, perhaps rather more than we bargained for. In either case we have the opportunity to begin to move.

However you continue, all that assumes a leisure where feelings are concerned which is rarely vouchsafed us. Feelings arrive and the balloon goes up. There is no space. And indeed, as I have consistently agreed, it is sometimes true that our feelings get the better of us and force their way into existence whether we like it or not. But by no means always. We can learn slowly to create space between the arousal of a feeling and its commission, not because we want to try and convert the feeling into something which shows us in a kinder light but because we want to use it constructively. We feel angry, yes, and in due course we may have to tell them so and why, but at the moment it does not seem to us that it would be helpful. So we decide to hold on to our anger for the time, a conscious decision intelligently reached.

It is worth mentioning one artifice we often use to avoid facing the disagreeable consequences of answering the question 'Who am I angry with?' because it would mean confrontation we do not care for. We say, 'I am really angry with myself.' It is often true as a first understanding of our anger. We are frustrated because we feel soldered to the spot, unable to move and angry with ourselves at our impotence. Very frequently though, lying a little way behind that anger and concealed by it, is a greater fury at some larger figure in our life who has hitherto always been too strong for us. It is that shadowy figure that we need to get to grips with, leaving our introverted anger behind us.

In handling our anger, then, we first acknowledge that the anger is true and then we make some attempt to elucidate it, paying particular attention to the true object of our anger. The next step, I would suggest, is to put our anger where it belongs. Too often we are afraid of the people who really make us angry and we offload our resentment on those who are closer to hand whose complaisance and whose loyalty we can usually rely upon.

I recall a lady who worked in an office where most of her fellow-workers were men. She was more highly qualified than most of the men, shrewd and intelligent. At work the men treated her as if she were the office girl. They would ask her to run errands for them, failed to consult her on any significant changes in office practice, assume she would make the coffee for them all and never commend her for any of the competent work that she performed. She fumed. Day after day she would return home from the office and complain bitterly to her husband. The men were chauvinists, nobody took her seriously, the job was lousy, she did the job better than most of the men, she never wanted to go back there again. The atmosphere of the home each evening was sour and embittered.

One evening as she was rambling on, her husband, who had always hitherto listened patiently and made soothing noises, decided that he had had enough. He reflected that what happened to his wife at work was nothing to do with him and everything to do with her. He was not causing any of the troubles she complained of and there was no reason in the world why he should be the recipient of all her jaundiced pique. So he turned on her and told her so. If she wanted to be angry, he said, then for heaven's sake take it out on those who were the cause of her anger and not on him. He was tired of his home being made unbearable each evening from causes that lay quite outside it.

They were both somewhat overwhelmed by this unexpected outburst and went thoughtfully to bed. Next day she returned from work, her eyes sparkling. 'I've done it!' she exclaimed. She had told them firmly that if they wanted coffee making or errands running then they had better do it themselves. She wasn't going to do it any more. Her work was as sound as theirs and she had plenty of ideas for changes in office practice. She was their equal in most respects and their superior in some.

The atmosphere at home was immediately lightened and transformed because her anger was no longer being dumped where it did not belong. Loving-kindness could now resume. On the other hand the atmosphere at work did not at once come to resemble what it had been like at home, as one might have expected. On the contrary because she had now laid claim to the professionalism and the equality which was rightfully hers her colleagues, after registering the shock of her new behaviour, almost immediately took her at her own now proved estimation of herself and began to treat her as the partner she was. Now that her justifiable anger had been placed where it rightfully belonged peace was restored in office and home.

We have another fear, however, that we need to examine before we finish with anger. It is the fear, often based on genuine grounds, that to express our anger will be destructive, and if there is a possibility that it might destroy us are we justified in risking it?

Let us acknowledge first that anger can be marvellously freeing. Long ago I rejoiced in the discovery of a splendid poem by Stevie Smith concerning a raven which had become stuck in a room with only three walls and was helplessly trying to find the way out. First she tried to release it with love.

> I took my raven by the hand, Oh come, I said, my Raven,
> And I will take you by the hand and you shall fly to heaven.
>
> But oh he sobbed and oh he sighed and in a fit he lay
> Until two fellow ravens came and stood outside to say:
>
> You wretched bird, conceited lump
> You well deserve to pine and thump.
>
> See how a wonder, mark it well
> My bird rears up in angry spell,

Oh do I then? he says, and careless flies
O'er flattened wall at once to heaven's skies.

And in my dream I watched him go
And I was glad, I loved him so,

Yet when I woke my eyes were wet
To think that Love had not freed my pet,

Anger it was that won him hence
As only Anger taught him sense.

Often my tears fall in a shower
Because of Anger's freeing power.[2]

So it was in the end the spur of anger which released the raven, just as it was the spur of anger which released not only the lady in the office but all those in office and home whom her lack of courage had been shackling. It was also the husband's anger which had initiated the process of healing in the first place, anger which some Christian traditions might have seen as a denial of Christian love but which in practice led to its restoration.

Christians need to acknowledge that anger has a rightful and effective place in God's design. It cuts through to the truth more quickly than hours of discussion. It frees tangled knots in human relationships. It cuts bullies down to size. It brings sudden silences in which reality can reassert itself. It liberates the soul.

It will nearly always be hurtful, or at least we always fear it will be hurtful, nor do I think we should avoid it on that account. 'I don't want to say anything', we declare, 'because I would only get angry and that would hurt him and where would that get us?' It would get us to the cause of the hurt. There lies between us, for some reason it may be hard to fathom until we release it in anger, a barrier which it will be painful to break through. In a dispensation which has a cross as its main symbol it would be hard to deny that such pain is not infrequently inevitable. New life arrives only as the old dies and dying is a painful business. Of all people Christians should not fear the bruises.

We need to be prepared for anger to hurt. Yet it can rarely be right for us to set out to hurt deliberately, a very different attitude to a yielding to the inescapable. Bullies are not acceptable among Christians but are often to be found there wielding their doctrinal cudgels, bellowing their disinterested virtues or picking at the church's open sores.

Nor can it be for our sake that we express our anger. Though we may accept with delight as a gift of grace that voicing our anger may free us for care and affection, people may not be used for our own ends, for that is a denial of love. Nor lastly must we flinch from the hurts that we shall undoubtedly receive in our turn, exposed as we shall be to the truth that anger produced on both sides. To expect others to hear the truth when we are still trying to dodge it is cowardly conduct.

So there are several dangerous traps along the road of anger, and the worst of all is the recognition that, anger or no, expressed or not, we are in certain respects trapped altogether. We are that blessed raven in the room, only this time the room has four walls, a roof and a ceiling and we shall never escape. The inevitable surrounds us on all sides and we waste our energy if we beat our wings in futile and painful anger against the unyielding boundaries.

We are born with certain characteristics, brought up to relate in certain ways, presented with only limited gifts, able to choose just a few paths, surrounded by people who may never change, live in communities that are ruled in styles we may not approve by authorities we have not elected, suffer the inflexibilities of all human life. We need to reserve our anger for those small chinks in the walls through which we can learn to be at least partly free.

6

The Feeling and the Fact

Thus far we have been examining the effect our views of emotions have upon the way we deal with them. I have suggested that one of the reasons we find emotions so acutely painful is because we blame ourselves when we find ourselves possessed of feelings we judge bad. We have to bear not only the fact that we are angry with, or hate, somebody but also the sense of guilt at having such a feeling at all. We should not be angry. We must not hate. We are doubly evil: for hating and for not being able to stop it.

I have argued that we are adding unnecessary burdens upon ourselves. Emotions are morally neutral. No emotion is either good or bad in itself. It is not wrong to feel angry since we have no means of making an emotion arrive or go away. We cannot congratulate ourselves because we feel loving towards somebody we normally find odious since the love was an unexpected and unheralded visitor. Our responsibility begins only at the point where we discover that the visitor has taken up residence and we have to decide what to do with it.

In discussing our loving and our anger I have made practical suggestions about the responsible actions we might begin to take. I have discussed how we can, without hypocrisy, act in a loving way whatever our feelings happen to be, and have looked at the irruption of sexuality into our love. In dealing with anger I have ventilated a couple of unhelpful devices we often use for evading anger and have offered a procedure for handling our resentments.

You may still be saying to yourselves, however, 'That's all very well, but what you have been describing so far is largely a series of internal processes. It is what I feel about my own feelings. I still can't quite see what I ought to do in a practical way. I mean, it is nearly always other people who are involved in my emotions – I'm jealous of this one, in love with that one, and furious with the other. So what do I do about *them?*'

This chapter and the next attempt to address that problem. In chapter 7 we shall be looking at it from the point of view of those who will persist in thinking of our emotions entirely in terms of how we can control them – the bludgeon approach. After laying down cautions about such a quest, that chapter will pick up and reinforce what I wish to make the main focus of this chapter. Here I want to demonstrate that our main weapon for resolving our emotional problems is to test out what we feel in the arena of the real world.

I call it the Feeling and the Fact and will illustrate it by returning again to our young friend, Jane Eyre.

Jane had found herself at an early age an orphaned and penniless child lodged in the home of a reluctant foster-mother and her deplorable children, rich relations of Jane's who treated her with no respect, gave her no affection and were only waiting for the day when they could pack her off to boarding school. The children teased her without mercy, the mother bullied her and the servants treated her as 'the scapegoat of the nursery'. A child of great passion, she deeply resented these injustices and had nobody with whom she could share her hurt.

In the absence of confirmatory evidence she began to wonder whether what was said of her was true. 'My habitual mood of humiliation, self-doubt, forlorn depression, fell damp on the embers of my decaying ire. All said I was wicked, and perhaps it might be so.'[1] Since the outer facts that surrounded her were thrown into continual doubt she was condemned to that loneliness which comes to those who lose touch with the realities of the outer world.

At the same time she could not be sure that her inner life was not playing her false too. She was afflicted by 'self-doubt'. All the adults about her forbade or repudiated her emotions and there was therefore no way that she could tell if they were true either. She was not of an age when rationality had yet much sway so she was the victim of her fantasies, and it was above all necessary for her that she should put both her inner and the outer world to the test.

The day came when she was left alone with her aunt some weeks after her unnerving sojourn in the locked room. She determined to say what she felt. She said to her aunt:

'I am not deceitful: if I were, I should say I loved *you*, but I declare I do not love you: I dislike you the worst of anybody in the world except John Reed; and this book about the liar, you may give it to your girl, Georgiana, for it is she who tells lies, and not I.'

This may not have been very tactful or even kind, but it immediately had the effect of laying open to verification her inner emotional world ('I do not love you ... or John Reed') and the outer factual one ('It is Georgiana who tells lies, and not I'). The effect on Mrs Reed was to produce an icy silence which Jane went on to fill with further similar statements from both worlds (the feeling: 'the very thought of you makes me sick', and the fact: 'you treated me with miserable cruelty'). She finishes like this:

'It is the *truth*. You think I have no feelings, and that I can do without one bit of love or kindness; but I cannot live so: and you have no pity. I shall remember how you thrust me back – roughly and violently thrust me back – into the red-room and locked me up there, to my dying day ... And that punishment you made me suffer because your wicked boy struck me – knocked me down for nothing. I will tell anybody who asks me questions this exact tale.'[1]

The word 'truth' is italicized in Charlotte Bronte's text. For this is the essence of the story. The truth, 'the exact tale' as Jane perceived it, was now out in the open. Her aunt could have taken the opportunity to reveal both how she felt (her feelings) and what her version of 'the exact tale' was (the fact). In the event she did neither and stayed silent, though her attitude to Jane became immediately and markedly more conciliatory. So far then as anybody was willing to verify them, the facts were established and feelings on at least Jane's side were expressed. The result for one of the participants was as follows:

Ere I had finished this reply, my soul began to expand, to exult, with the strangest sense of freedom, of triumph, I ever felt. It seemed as if an invisible bond had burst, and that I had struggled out into unhoped-for liberty.[2]

Soon after, Jane had pangs of remorse over her outspokenness, but she decided she would not retract a word of it since it was so manifestly true and Mrs Reed had not taken the opportunity to contradict it. An indication that her boldness had brought about a real change in her was revealed in a remark made by Bessie, the maid, in a conversation shortly afterwards, 'You've got quite a new way of talking.'

That is the sort of process I am referring to when I talk of the feeling and the fact.

Until she spoke Jane was in great danger. Children through their lack of experience find it very hard to put themselves in other people's shoes and consequently have a desperately tragic and isolated view of their existence. She may have distorted the facts of the Reed's alleged cruelty and she certainly failed to counterbalance those facts with others that were in the Reeds' favour. What had actually happened needed to be firmly established and since there was not, and rarely is, any independent witness, the only way open to Jane and Mrs Reed was to create circumstances in which the participants, so far as they were able, could agree the facts. To establish what happened was the only way that Jane could be sure she was not suffering from a hysterical persecution fantasy. If she had wished to, Mrs Reed could have responded with her version of the facts. The fact that she did not was an indication that, as so often in such circumstances, she immediately recognized the truth when she heard it.

If the facts needed testing so did the feelings. As always Jane's feelings gave a confused jumble of messages. She was depressed and lonely, felt a hatred for Mrs Reed and her children and above all had a powerful sense of injustice, that is, she could not see the facts as presented by others matched the way that she saw them. Guilt is always an accompaniment of such feelings as, in the absence of facts, we readily blame ourselves for our condition.

Out of this tangle Jane chose to express the emotions that were most pressing, her hatred and her sense of injustice. She immediately discovered that her depression and her loneliness, her self-doubt and guilt were fellow-travellers to her anger which all vanished as soon as the anger was out in the open. The reaction she observed in Mrs Reed, and later in Bessie, was confirmation that her feelings too had a real and not merely an imaginary life. There were facts in the outer world to which her feelings related.

She had then accomplished the first two essential tasks, validating the independent reality both of the outer facts and of the inner feelings by bringing them out into the open. The matching of these two realities, the point at which she dared to move out of her interior life and risk its encounter with another human being, came when she decided to act, to confront Mrs Reed with what she felt and what she knew. It is always so. The inter-dependence of the facts and the feelings is verified and illuminated in the crucible of the real world.

As we shall see in the next chapter, it is not always sensible or appropriate to share our emotions directly with the person concerned, as Jane did. More often than not, it is. Saying what we feel clarifies what is true in fact and feeling alike.

Let us imagine, since it is a common enough occurrence, that we have been burdened for many years by something that has gone wrong between ourselves and our mother. It is quite hard, we find, to put our finger on it. It seems to be an accumulation of things, or perhaps one rather dread, hidden distortion upon which every subsequent misunderstanding has been built. We are still fond of her, have a high regard for her, recognize that she reared us with what care and affection she was capable of, yet she sometimes makes us want to scream.

She comes to stay in our house and shows her strong dis-approval of the way we bring up our children. She may not say very much but we know her well and all that we need to hear to make us grind our teeth is the sharp drawing in of breath as we commit what she believes to be yet another folly. Occasionally we say in exasperation, 'Oh, mother!' but quickly shut our mouths because we do not want to hurt her. We long for her to leave and when she does we kiss her with tears in our eyes, feeling guilty because we both do and do not want her.

More often than not we give some relief to this great churning around of emotions inside us by nagging away at our spouses or children who, like the husband in an earlier chapter whose wife was having a rotten time at work, feel put upon because they have an inkling the business is nothing to do with them.

It is a confused tangle, just like Jane Eyre's, and we shall need to give some careful attention to it. There are always the two elements in that sort of relationship, the fact and the feeling. There is the memory we have of incidents that have happened over the years between ourselves and our mother. These, so far as we are concerned, are the facts. They may not, however, be accurate recollections.

A few weeks ago, long after I had written the chapter where I sketched my early childhood and described myself as 'quiet, shy, diffident', I came upon an old school report of mine when I would have been about seven years old. To my utter amazement the report said words to the effect, 'If only Hugh wouldn't talk so much, he would be capable of good work.' I have still absolutely no recollection of having been a chatterbox at that age (I certainly wasn't after I became a teenager) yet the evidence is irrefutable that for at least one stage of my life I got it wrong.

We may have got it wrong. Time or temper may have distorted our memories. Moreover there is another side to the facts of the situation, our mother's. She will have her own memories and because she was in a different relationship to us from ours to her, they will be at least marginally different. They may be unbelievably different, as my own were. No matter. The paramount concern is that we should begin to share the facts, being prepared for amazed looks and, 'But it wasn't a bit like that!' and 'I didn't intend to do that at all!'

And then there are the feelings. We sometimes settle for a discussion about the facts because we prefer to avoid the feelings. Those feelings in us though have not gone away, are always in danger of bursting through. Because at the time those events did (or of course did not) happen some kind of feeling was attached to every event. We were devastated and felt abandoned when mother went into hospital for two months and nobody explained where she had gone. We were totally indifferent to her when she returned home but would also like to have hit her if we had dared. Or we were, we half suspect smugly, the favoured one in the family and were always taken to school personally by mother, so why was that foul elder sister of ours always tagging along behind when she could easily have gone on her own.

Most parents are good enough at parenting. We do not need to have had a rotten mother for these sort of feelings to be around, and indeed it is doubtful that we would, to begin with, be able to identify them as accurately as these examples show. It is quite possible too that the feelings are based upon a misunderstanding at the time. Mother's feelings are relevant to what happened. She may have made supreme efforts to keep in touch with us from her hospital bed and have given all manner of treats when she returned. Without our being the least aware of it, she could have been feeling full of guilty remorse that she had had to abandon her child for a time.

I need, I think, pursue the picture no longer. We have at least two people involved, each of whom will have their version of the facts with different feelings attached to those facts. Nothing of the past is likely to be elucidated, none of the feelings then or now is likely to be healthily evaluated and released until one or another of us have the courage to begin talking.

The strongest inhibition that prevents us from doing so is the fear of hurting others, though we sometimes use that as a respectable excuse for not wanting to hurt ourselves. 'I *can't* tell her what I feel. She would feel so dreadful.' I'm afraid she probably will, and so will we. There is no way that such ancient hurts can be honestly faced without pain and sorrow. The reason for this naturally is that they are not really ancient at all, for their effects dog our relationship with one another every day of our lives.

It is made easier for us if we make a sympathetic attempt to put ourselves in our mother's shoes. Hopelessly selfish as we are, we often forget what it might have been like, what it might still be like, for her. She may be as sad as we are that she cannot break free from being our mother and see us at last as an adult. Can we picture what sort of marriage she might have had all those years, its joys and deficiencies? Putting ourselves in her world, without withdrawing from the painful task of encounter, brings warmth with which to soften the hurts.

The fact and the feeling. These are the two entities with which we are involved in our emotional lives and they must be neither confused nor separated. If we do not maintain a firm hold upon the independent reality of what has happened we can easily be driven into an interior desolation where we are entirely on our own and nothing is true. If we do not give our trust to, really believe in, the feelings which we discover in ourselves we shall in the end so devalue our interior life that the person who is 'I' becomes lost, perhaps for ever. And we must not be deflected from our – not always successful – attempts to match our interior realities with the outer lest we fall into fantasy on the one hand or a barren rationality on the other.

Having arrived thus far, it would not be surprising if there was still some confusion in our minds. We may still not be able to see quite how the feeling and the fact are to be distinguished, or indeed how they relate. They seem to shift around. We think we have got hold of the fact that mother favoured us until we meet our sister who says that no, as a matter of fact she was the favourite. The fact then immediately turns into a feeling of rivalry. When mother is appealed to so that we may know what really happened, she stumbles and stalls because she either does not wish to hurt either of our feelings or she has never really been able to sort out which of us she favours. She doesn't know any longer what is fact and feeling.

We should not be in the least anxious about that. We are dealing with complicated matters. When we wish to clarify them a little more, as I have said, the most hopeful way forward is to bring the feelings out into the open and to give everybody a chance to share their feelings and to check them out against the facts.

But it might be helpful for those of you who would like to tease out some of the difficulties rationally if I spent the rest of this chapter illustrating how closely fact and feeling are intertwined. It will not be simply an intellectual game. We often start in our thinking from certain presuppositions which have a limited number of outcomes. We take a lot for granted. There are strictly practical reasons in this field why we should examine more closely what we normally take for granted. Our behaviour depends upon what we think about our lives.

For example, let us suppose that we suffer from recurrent bouts of depression, accompanied by headaches, loss of appetite and insomnia. Maybe we are of the opinion that our depression, an emotional state, is a chemical dysfunction. We go to the doctor and say, 'Please will you give me some librium' or whatever. One day, we believe, the drugs will be effective and we shall recover. Or maybe we go for a psychological approach. We create for ourselves, we believe, the physical tensions that produce depression and headaches. So we go off to seek relaxation therapy, foot massage or yoga. Perhaps we think that depression is a sign of unfaithfulness; we are somehow refusing to let God into our lives. In this case we go and speak to our minister and prepare ourselves for the laying on of hands. And if we are convinced that all depressive states are simply 'in the mind', we will tell ourselves to snap out of it and will take plenty of vigorous exercise and wholemeal bread.

What action we take to manage our depression depends precisely upon what we believe about it. For that very practical reason we need to keep re-examining our convictions.

So what do we believe about the emotions? What kind of reality are they? The extraordinary range of language we use is a first indication of how finely they are woven into the fabric of our whole existence. We need to express a tremendous number of attitudes to our emotions and we have to try to find words to say it. Let us look for a moment at four different types of language we use – language of pictures, of the body, of the mind and of pure speculation.

'He is a warmly affectionate person, but she is very cold.' That is metaphorical language, picture language. We are not talking about people's respective properties of heat but of the way we find them. Or we say, 'I was deeply hurt' and 'He is a shallow sort of a fellow.' Again it is the language of illustration taken from the images of water. We are so familiar with this way of speaking that it scarcely ever occurs to us that we are only approximating to what we mean to describe. Feelings and emotions are not actually shallow or hot, it is just – and here we go again – a deeply significant way of speaking about them.

Another kind of language we use all the time is physiological, body language. We shall come back in a little while to the implication of this. Here we are only looking at what we say. 'I could smell the fear on him', a man might remark of another he successfully challenges. 'When she refused to do what I told her to, I saw red' is a way of describing our anger. We use a great deal of language derived from the internal organs. 'I saw a stunningly beautiful girl in the high street this morning and my stomach turned over', or 'My heart went out to those poor children suffering from famine in Africa', or of a person who shows courage, 'I'll give her that, she shows guts.' This way of speaking is not in the least modernistic or peculiar to our language, as we can see for instance from the frequency with which the Bible talks of (in the authorized translation) 'bowels of compassion'.

Psychological language is a strange phenomenon. My edition of the Shorter Oxford Dictionary describes psychological in this way: 'Of or pertaining to the science of the nature, functions and phenomena of the human soul or mind'. 'Soul or mind', there's a distinct hedging of bets if you like! Nobody can agree what raw material psychology precisely handles, yet we use the words all the time. Sometimes it is to give a sort of scientific verisimilitude to feelings we know about. We use phobia instead of fear and trauma for feeling hurt inside. We say men are impotent and women frigid, referring only partly to their sexual behaviour. 'The chap was a real schizo / paranoid about spiders / a nervous wreck / a masochist with his pupils.' Psychological language is very hard to define because it shades off in one direction towards metaphor ('wreck' from the sea, 'frigid' from the properties of heat) and in the other to the last form of speaking I want to refer to, the metaphysical.

Metaphysical language is a form of speculation. We invent words to describe things which have no material existence, like being, cause, identity or time. These concepts relate to what we know about but we cannot, so to speak, put our finger on them. I have already referred to the motions as 'deep-seated forces', have talked of 'what is outside and what is inside' and have tried to describe 'several different "I"s wandering around inside us'. All such language is metaphysical. 'Force' does not refer to anything physical any more than I intend to refer to a tangible 'inside' or 'outside'. These concepts, and others like power or energy or resistance, are taken from a physical scientific world which is itself finding materiality harder and harder to pin down. They are also words that we cannot avoid when we talk about our feelings and emotions.

So how are we to speak intelligently of emotion? The way that I have chosen is this. I intend to begin with the very simplest examples of what we would all agree to be feelings and upon that foundation to see if we can make some progress. As a prelude to this I think I need to say, because you may have wondered, that I do not make any sharp division between feelings and emotions, except in a strictly limited physical sense as we shall see in a moment. Both words affirm, as I have described it, 'the mainspring of our reality as human beings'. Both words can be used of those tendencies of our beings which we identify individually as fear, love, sadness, guilt and so on. I take emotion to be intensified feeling, and passion to be an even more intensified emotion.

In my first example I come up to you and stick a knife into your arm. You feel pain, nobody has any doubt about that. It is in essence a feeling entirely lacking in complication, a purely physical reaction to sharp steel cutting into flesh. It might be simpler if we regularly used the word 'sensation' to describe this reaction, for there are no emotional overtones, nothing that makes it distinctively a feeling in our use of the word. This is, in my view, the only use of the word feeling which differs widely from the word emotion.

However, the sensation in your arm is likely to be accompanied swiftly by various emotional responses. Depending on how far your physical hurt demands your full attention, you are likely to feel angry with me and to be afraid of me. How these are expressed will depend upon factors inside yourself. If you have been brought up, for example, by a violent father you have never come to terms with, your fear will probably outweigh your anger and you will cower before me. Your anger, though unexpressed, will not of course disappear. Feelings cannot be so easily dissipated. Probably you will take it out later on your family or on the nurse who bandages your arm and they will wonder what has got into you.

I meanwhile may be feeling excited that I have dared to do what one part of me has been longing to do for years, or contrariwise thoroughly shocked at an action of which I thought I was totally incapable. These emotions I shall take home with me and my family will soon be embroiled with them. Embroiled in different ways naturally, depending upon their own experiences and reactions to violence itself and to the fact that it is I, a known and hitherto relatively affable fellow, who has displayed such an unexpected side of his character.

Here is another example from the gentler side of the emotions. A teenage girl is hungry, tells her mother so and her mother gives her something to eat. That is an unambiguous transaction in which hunger is satisfied. On the other hand the daughter and her mother have a long history of relationship, and how the mother presents the food and how the girl receives it will be a

small cameo of that history. Since the day of her birth the giving
and receiving or witholding of food has been the coinage of
their interaction. To offer the breast has been to offer love and
to be refused is to be rejected. A meal, even all these years later,
still carries with it the emotional exchanges which they have both
lived with. The tray of food may be offered and accepted with a
quiet smile on both sides. Or, even all these years later, the
mother may offer it in anxious anticipation of rejection and
the girl receive it with the sullenness of long-remembered
disappointment.

My point is that the most ordinary events, and particularly
transactions between two or more people, carry with them not
only a range of emotions which arise directly out of the event
itself but also a history of emotion within all the participants and
in those to whom each of them relate. This is why people so
regularly and wonderingly say after some thunderous row, 'It
was only a silly little thing that caused it.' The accidentally
smashed cup or the ten minutes we are late for an appointment
carry an intensity of feeling only marginally related to the event,
and we will often be the recipients of high emotion out of
proportion to what has happened and in fact not always any
concern of ours whatsoever.

No event in which sentient beings are involved – and I say
'sentient beings' because I am unwilling entirely to exclude the
higher animals from the world of emotions – is a simple event.
Even those which look most clinical have an emotional com-
ponent. You would not think that to set and heal a broken leg or
to take out an appendix would be anything but an unemotional
process, yet the television companies never tire of the hospital
as a hotbed of emotional crises. Laboratory experiments are
carried out in strict scientific sequences by specialists who wax
furious with their rivals and their assistants, fear that their
research will fail, envy the director who is paid more money
and fall in love with the technician. No one can pretend that
their experiments will be quite unaffected by their emotional
turmoils.

Events then in the sentient world are all accompanied by
feelings which belong as much to the past as to the present and
become thereby, in view of the number of people ultimately
affected by the event, ever more complex. Emotions may initially arrive as an intense single experience, like falling in love, but

they soon stack up like planes waiting to land at a busy airport. Falling in love is followed by guilt because the object of our love is impermissible, then jealousy because of the others whose love is also focussed there, and fear because of the possible consequences, and outbursts of anger or appalled anguish with the one we have loved for many years hitherto, and many other emotions all of which touch down in random sequence.

Just as events in the outer world carry a feeling or a jumble of feelings from the inner world so it is true of our bodies. Our bodies affect, and are affected by, what we are feeling inside. Indeed I think it is true to say that our bodies are one of the most valuable clues of all in interpreting our emotions.

At its simplest it is what we all know as 'mind over matter'. We are thoroughly enjoying a plate of stew until our host suddenly tells us that it is mostly composed of slugs, did we know? Most of us will stop eating and some of us will be physically sick. The idea of slugs is enough for our stomachs to tighten against or even physically to eject what until that moment we were appreciating. Or there is that strange affliction called tachycardia when the heart suddenly starts pumping very fast, sending the blood racing round the body. It is, I understand, physically without long-term danger to the subject, can usually be stopped by applying pressure to exactly the right spot on the body and is brought about entirely by mental stress of one kind or another. A pumping mechanism is directly affected by what we are feeling.

The fact also of course works the other way round so that by means of drugs or alcohol we can induce states of equilibrium or release which can be effective against anxiety, depression or manic behaviour. A change in our emotional state can be brought about directly by a change in our bodily state, but, as the medical profession is fully aware, the process is not predictable from one patient to the next which indicates that other factors are also at work.

There is a certain correlation between some emotions and some bodily states. If we are standing on top of a 150-foot church tower and somebody jostles us so that we nearly lose our footing certain physical changes will come about in our body. We shall grow cold because the blood vessels contract in order to increase the blood supply to the muscles so that we can cope better with the danger. We will also find that 'our stomach turns over' because digestive activities are suddenly being halted in order to mobilize the body to withstand the sudden assault. What we feel is fear, and afterwards we can equally well say, 'My blood ran cold' as 'I was afraid'. We are quite clear that the danger, though physically expressed, is not primarily related to the body because we do not ask for a doctor but for somebody to escort us back down the steps as quickly as possible.

However, there is no exact correlation between our bodies and our emotions. If somebody is afraid we cannot predict whether they will stand and shake, freeze rigidly, run away, vomit, put their hands to their mouth and scream or be apparently quite unmoved.

There is an interrelation between events and our emotions and between our bodies and our emotions. It seems somehow as if the feelings and emotions do not live on their own but are manifested between certain boundaries of our existence. Let us consider this with respect to the strange phenomenom of music.

Music can be, and often is, a carrier of emotion. It is difficult to know what to call it. We can't term it as bodily though it is our bodies that hear it and sometimes respond emotionally to it, and it is solid instruments that produce it. It isn't quite an event; it seems a little more substantial than that for it has time but no space. Since it is carried from one place to another on what we are pleased to call waves it is only possible to think of music in responsorial terms. It happens between and within. But between and within what? I think we shall have to say that it is between the instruments that produce the music on the one side, the church organ, guitars, human voice, orchestra, saxaphone or drums, and the needs in us which respond to such instruments on the other, the needs to find unity with our fellows, to establish an identity, to give rein to our interior being sometimes in a bodily way, to discover or to maintain a personal, corporate or national history.

It is at the boundaries of such events that the importance of music arises for our emotional lives, sometimes beneficially, sometimes malignly. For example the main purpose of a military band is to induce a fervent bond of unity between soldiers which will make it possible for them to act in ways which as rational individuals they could well find repugnant. It is to this extent a manipulative exercise and its worst manifestation is the deliberate use of martial music to bring a crowd into a state of subjugation to another's will. Some of the wilder religious sects are well-known to practise such villainous behaviour. On the other hand if we have been brought up with Bach, Beethoven and Tchaikowsky ringing in our ears, the record we choose when we sit down to listen will to some degree be an emotional response to – and sometimes a deliberate raising of the emotional temperature towards – other events that are going on in our lives at the moment, and to what we remember such music meant to us in the past. We might choose the 1812 Overture if we are angry with our father-in-law or one of Beethoven's later string quartets if we are grieving for a friend, even though we may not be consciously aware of the reasons for our choice.

Memories which are an accumulation in our interior beings of real or imagined events that have happened to us and their real or imagined consequences, play a significant part in our musical experience. Whether it be lullabies and nursery songs, national anthems, raucous pub songs or old, familiar hymns, they help us to recall our personal histories and to relive them again, re-establishing our identities and our partnerships. So music, which is a phenomenon peculiar to itself, can be seen to be another mediator of our emotions, relating to, but not encompassed by, both the events that happen and our bodies the events happen to.

I began my attempt at explaining emotions and feelings with an example of simple sensation, a knife pushed into your arm. Never can we escape from these facts of our existence which, as we have seen, in some odd way carry our emotions. Emotion does not live in a vacuum. It is not, as the Brute family thought, 'a little lost feeling in a field of daisies'. Emotion always lies in relation to something or someone in the outer world. The fact in the outer world will always be the same but the relationship to it will be different for each individual and frequently for the same individual at different times.

A sharp knife is a fact. Lying on a plate beside a plum cake it is one thing. Pointed at our throat by a frenzied chef it is another. When it is revealed that the chef is really a disguised friend playing the fool, it is another thing again.

In sum then we can say that feelings, which are common to mankind in their diversity but belong in each case distinctively and uniquely to an individual, are always attached to some concrete reality in the world. This reality may be a thing like a knife, or an event like a motor accident, or a body as when we shake with fear or weep for sadness, or a person like the child whose loving smile, as we say, 'melts me', or any combination of these. It can also, rather confusingly, be an event or a person we have taken inside ourselves, as when we spend energy having internal battles with a long-deceased overbearing parent who still lives in us because we have not dealt with what they represent.

Emotion is like a bridge.[3] There is the fact of ourselves on one side of the bridge and the fact of the world to which we relate on the other. Our emotions unite us to the world or, if we refuse them, separate us from the world. That is the pathway upon which the two realities become one in us.

What I have tried to do in this chapter is to help us find ways of using that bridge to unite us to a world which is real in fact and in feeling. Bridges are best walked on. We need to test them out and risk the attempt to cross one. We need to say what we feel. As Jane Eyre discovered, the rewards are always unmistakable:

> Ere I had finished this reply, my soul began to expand, to exult, with the strongest sense of freedom, of triumph, I ever felt. It seemed as if an invisible bond had burst, and that I had struggled out into unhoped-for liberty.

7

The Control of the Emotions

When I see the title of this chapter, my boyhood returns to me. I see the teacher who frightened me so much, his head cocked to one side, regarding me with a peculiar intensity, daring me to step for a single moment out of line. I see the look my mother gave me if a swear word slipped out, and guilt swept over me. I remember the wicked delight I silently enjoyed when I threw a flowerpot dangerously at my brother and it was he who was roundly rebuked for his misbehaviour. I hear my friends remarking coldly, 'Oh, don't be so childish!' or 'Grow up!' when cheerfulness took hold of me and I pranced madly round the room or fell into helpless giggles. I recall the first time, in my early twenties, that I heard a Franciscan friar talking about Christ and being dumbfounded to believe it possible that God might be for me rather than against me.

Not that my upbringing was in any way markedly severe. Far from it. It was just that there were boundaries carefully maintained by my elders and peers within which all our activities had to take place. Or, to use another analogy, I was told that I had to be disciplined, and better still self-disciplined, keeping a rein on all those parts of me which might lead me into immoral or unseemly behaviour. If I could not keep such a rein on myself then somebody else would have to do it for me.

Somehow it was always my emotions that were the subject of such strictures. It was my emotions that were always running away with me or that everybody thought might run away with me. I was allowed to be a little angry, in fact they would sometimes smile at a really good tantrum because it was so unlike my usual behaviour. But they set limits of their own choosing to such conduct and would soon say, 'Now that's enough' and I would have to rein myself in even though my anger may not have run its course. Being shy with girls, I was positively encouraged later on to take an interest in the opposite sex. 'Now there's a nice girl', they would say of some neighbouring beauty and I would smirk or glower. Yet I was left in no doubt that I should treat all girls with the respect that I owed, and sometimes gave, my sisters and I was not invited, as they would say knowingly and mysteriously, 'to take it too far'.

I was led to believe that it was my emotions that were the seat of immorality. Of course it was wrong if I did not say my prayers at night or did not go to church on Sundays or failed to do my schoolwork each day but it did not feel quite as wrong in the commission of the act as in the implications of disobedience behind it. I was wrong not chiefly because I failed to do such things but more because I had not obeyed those who had a right to expect me to do them. I was self-willed and stubborn, they said, and it was not too long before I was almost forced into confrontation. I became angry then or sullen and it was at this point that I really felt bad, at the point when feelings that arose in me came into conflict with the expectations of those about me. It was more immoral to feel angry and sullen than it was not to say my prayers or do my homework. That may not have been their intention but that is what it felt like.

Other emotions were not so much immoral as tedious and wretched feelings which were better avoided if I could. When I cried at the unutterably sad prospect of leaving home for a time they would eye my tears regretfully, recognizing my unhappiness but hoping that I might soon pull myself together. 'You'll enjoy it once you are there,' they would urge, leaping forward a few days so that the emotional present could be left behind. I pounded my pillow in solitary misery in my bedroom, striving to restrain my tears downstairs.

In contrast to these sort of 'control yourself' experiences, which younger people than I may recognize in a slightly different form, it was as if there had always been, or people always feared there might be, families or individuals in whom there was no control at all. Often identifying a particular family of their acquaintance, they deplored and feared behaviour which did not seem to have any boundaries whatsoever. Emotions ran wild, right and wrong seemed to have no meaning and nobody claimed any morals.

Such people fell into different categories. There were those few who were pathologically disturbed and posed danger to their neighbours and everybody was relieved when they fell into the hands of the hospitals or the law courts. Others caused no damage to anybody else but seemed to live in a permanent anguish of soul because their behaviour and their emotions were quite ungoverned yet they constantly wished to be different. Seeking salvation, they often fell further and further into indulgence.

The ones most feared perhaps were those who lived by what appeared to be extraordinarily lax standards, who seemed to be happy in doing so and who showed no signs of guilt or a bad conscience. They slept with whom they liked, held frenzied parties, robbed everyone except their friends, never held down a job and seemed not to wish to exercise any control over the expression of what they felt.

Very likely much of all that was fantasy. After all we see people only from the outside and cannot know what sort of inner stresses they might carry. Yet it was and remains a powerful fantasy and one that makes us search anxiously for means of control. The emotions are like a wild donkey, this fantasy runs, which, unless it is kept tethered chewing away at the grass we have chosen for it, will race madly away, with us clinging to the rope, begging it to stop, not strong enough to restrain it, fearing disaster.

We need now therefore to spend some time considering ways in which we have been traditionally trained to exercise control over our emotions, to keep the donkey tethered. The first of these I shall look at is the encouragement of ascetical practices.

In the history of the church ascetical practice, deliberate physical sacrifices, have been a powerful presence. The picture of a Simeon Stylites, for instance, who sat in the open air on top of a pole for sixty years, offering gracious counsel to his admirers on feast days only, is a mighty spur to the imagination. Brother Lawrence offered spiritual riches from a monastery kitchen, so could we not at least make some small sacrifice for God? The urge to do something practical, to make a token

payment, to rein in our desires by a votive offering, is com-
pelling in human religious affairs and we have seen briefly in
chapter 2 that certain eras of the church have judged monastic
discipline to be the only path by which men and women may
reach that perfection which they have seen God to be demanding.
Indeed the word 'discipline' in some periods of monastic history
has meant the physical subjection of the body by various self-
inflicted means.

And so we may recall on our small scale the times we have
knelt bolt upright on a hard floor as we prayed, or refused to eat
certain dishes for a period or attempted a course of transcendental
meditation. In many different ways we have attempted to exercise some control over our bodies and souls. Lenten penances
used to be an invariable feature of church life though these days
ministers are likely to emphasize the positive side of sacrifice and
suggest that we might send to a charity the money we save by not
eating chocolates. Where formal penances linger on in those
churches which practise sacramental confession they tend to be
brief, not onerous and certainly not intended as any recompense
to God for sins committed.

Penances then are out of fashion, so maybe we are slowly
learning that the emotions, like all sentient things, do not lightly
yield to an act of war. As soon as the emotions see our hand
hovering over the scabbard they gather themselves to battle and
determine that they will not be overcome. Bludgeoned by a
ruthless Christian they will sink down with battered head and re-
emerge later, possibly in a different, more sinister, form. He
who refuses to allow himself to be jealous of his brother and
punishes himself for it with hours of prayer may feel the
jealousy disappear only to discover later that he is now indifferent to his brother or that there is a new, strange and
unexpected antagonism between his children. Emotions will not
be denied their presence in the world.

This is not by any means to deny that a life of discipline is out
of place for the Christian. That would be absurd. Little is
achieved without habits of time and concentration. What I am
saying is that the emotions will never yield in an adversarial
position. Any serious attempt to use asceticism to control our
emotions is likely to end in self-righteousness.

It should not be necessary in a Christian church to spend
much time in registering the futility of trying to handle our

emotions by means of authority or law. St Paul's experience on
the Damascus road (Acts 9.1–9) is definitive for the Christian in
the sense that it was there that he finally understood that,
although he had tried for a very long time, he could not make
himself righteous. The world was ruled by the graciousness of
God and all that was required of us was that we should slip into
that grace through faith. Salvation could not be earned by
keeping the law (Gal. 5.4–11) nor could emotions be controlled
by ascetical practices (Col. 2.20–23). Everything from God came
as a gift.

Yet we have seen that although it was Paul who made it certain
that the church could never again for long neglect that foundation stone in God's building of the world, it was also Paul who
tried to maintain it by the very means that contradicted it. He
used his authority to ensure the preservation of his perception
of the gospel and to claim control over the behaviour of those
who believed it (see chapter 2). Thereby he set up antagonism
which, by imitation, countless Christians have subsequently
fallen into.

So there are always those in the church, and many of them its
ministers, who feel that it is their business to exercise some kind
of control over their adherents' emotions. They use many
different sources of authority. Sometimes it resides in themselves as the carriers of the gospel, sometimes in the Bible
selectively interpreted, sometimes in the tradition of the church,
sometimes in natural law or the ten commandments or in a
benign implication that the minister will be offended by any
deviation. It is as if they fear for the grace of God which, in the
absence of other coercion, might not be strong enough to bring
about salvation. They keep wishing to act as the schoolmasters of
the law (Gal. 3.24,25) lest Christ might not bring us to faith. It is
permissible, they imply, to express any emotion which does not
offend such authority and can be contained, even flattered, by it
(tears, sadness, fear, love within certain contexts) but it is not
right to set up emotional challenges (anger, hatred, jealousy,
love in other contexts).

So used are so many of us since childhood to the acceptance
of such imperialism that we both receive it without question
(though with some resentment) and ourselves set up our own
internal policemen to do the job for us – and then wonder why
we are so frustrated. External authoritative suppression of our

natural desires is, as I have said, perfectly acceptable at home where children are beginning to learn their way about the world, though even there they should quickly be learning the priority of the graciousness of love over the enforcement of law. To allow our adult emotional lives to be controlled by laws or lawgivers will only perpetuate a childish faith which has not yet become responsible.

For the avoidance of misunderstanding again it is necessary to say here that authority is not eliminated or disqualified by such arguments. We visit a particular butcher for a number of reasons. He appears to us to have had a good training and to know his job and we do not expect to receive a chump chop if we ask for a piece of shin. He is also, we seem to feel, a man who is a natural butcher. He has, so to speak, butchery written all over him and we therefore trust him for his inherent qualities. He may also go out of his way to be pleasant to us, to meet us in friendliness and neighbourliness. All these qualities – his training, his charisma, his desire to be on our side – give him a real, practical authority. At times, since we are not skilled in butchery and do not have his special charisma, we shall willingly accept his authority on a variety of culinary matters. Moreover the availability of butchers, and especially of good butchers, is quite narrow and there is nowhere else to go for a knowledge of meat except the butcher. Within those very real limits we still in the end choose our butcher, select what advice we shall follow and choose our meat. Some authorities have simply to be endured; but we must choose as many as we can.

Neither asceticism nor external authorities then are much help in managing our emotions and many of us have understood that long ago. Yet emotions still crowd in, one on top of the other, and while we do not always have the capacity to cope they will not give us any rest. So a third way to gain some control of our emotions is to bury them inside ourselves. The technical term often used in pyschotherapeutic circles for this process is repression, which may be anything from a mild to a deeply serious disorder and the graver ones, as always, require professional help.

The most difficult repressions to manage are those which have become lodged in the unconscious, a part of our nature, most professionals seem to agree, that is not accessible to us under normal conditions. It is like a box of unremembered feelings or perhaps an accumulation of all our forgotten experiences, most of them things it is too uncomfortable for us to bring to mind or emotions we have not been allowed to feel.

We may not, for example, remember that our parents would never allow us to be afraid. We had maybe a period of enforced separation from them when we had to go into hospital as an infant and that trauma reappeared several times later. We would wake in the night and call for our mother and she would usually appear, often not quickly enough to satisfy us. Our father, if he came, would be cross and brusque and tuck us up quickly. We began to see frightening objects in the corner of the room and our parents pooh-poohed it. 'There's nothing there. It's your imagination again!' They became angry in the end and to avoid losing them altogether we acquiesced and the fear dropped into the unconscious. But as naughty children, locked in their bedroom, will sometimes climb out of the window and reappear making ugly faces at the adults, so the fears may reappear out of our unconscious later in strange phobias, not apparently connected. We dare not meet people in the street, we have to keep a light on all night, we are terrorized by spiders.

These repressions in the unconscious we are of course only vaguely, if at all, aware of and we do not have to assume that they are pathological. We are not responsible for their presence in us and we may be able to approach them step by step as we give our attention to repressions that we practise more consciously.

For frequently we just decide, more or less consciously, that we are not going to feel this, that or the other way any more. We suppress or control the feeling. On the surface that seems a positive and admirable thing to do if the feeling is judged to be a bad one. We have always, for instance, found David difficult to live with. Whenever we meet him we feel thoroughly hostile. So we decide to do something about it. When next we meet him we swallow our dislike, smile sweetly, discourse cheerfully and maybe receive a more positive response than we have ever had since he now feels a chink in our hostility. That has been a sort of control of our emotions, and the valuable part of it is that we have chosen to take the matter in hand.

All of us have to face the primacy of that point of choice. We are all able to choose. There may be times in our lives when circumstances are so overwhelming, such as when we are physically ill or hindered with urgent practicalities, that we cannot make choices at all in the real areas of our concern, and others when the choices we can make are only second-best because maybe our courage is not up to handling what we know we ought to do. Yet choice always remains potentially an option and it is choice that gets us moving.

We have now therefore chosen to approach David positively and already that may strike you as alarming in a different kind of way. I started with the word 'control' and have quickly arrived at the word 'choice'. Control feels internal, choosing involves movement. When we talk about the control of our emotions we picture a reining in, a thwarting of one part of oneself by another, a subjective act of the will, a tethering of the donkey. That intimidates us because we have little confidence that our will to control our feelings will be stronger than the feelings themselves. We will all have had melancholy proof of that in the past.

On the other hand choosing unnerves us because it means that we will need to leave the shelter of our inner battleground and risk ourselves in the open world of other people's feelings. There is no certainty at all that David will respond as enthusiastically as we would like, and he could easily take the opportunity of sliding a dagger through these welcome chinks in our armour. If we have controlled ourselves we should easily be able to parry such blows withdrawing behind our breastplate; if we have chosen, we are more vulnerable because we have willingly bared our breast. However, vulnerability, though painful, is, we may have discovered, more fruitful than living behind the armour. So it may be more helpful to move away from thinking about the control of our feelings and ponder what it might mean to choose to act.

What is it then that we have chosen to do about David? We have chosen to try and act differently. Now it is at this point that we must be absolutely clear what we are about. If we say to ourselves 'I will control my feelings about David' then the battle has become an internal one, probably bewildering to David who is unaware of our determination. And in all such inner battles there is an almost certain danger to our integrity, for we are presenting to ourselves that we feel differently from how we actually feel. We know we feel hostile, we say, 'I will not allow myself to feel hostile' and hostility immediately goes underground. It does not disappear, for feelings cannot be banished in this way. They bide their time or reappear elsewhere. Meanwhile we go blithely on, half or three-quarters believing that we have cracked it, anxious a little still because our feelings have not often proved to be compliant.

It is our integrity, our wholeness, that is at stake. We have deliberately divided ourselves up into two. We may relate famously with David from that moment but the mystery of our hostility will be unexplained and therefore potentially will be always ready to reassert itself with him or with somebody else.

In my view, as you know, it is no fault of ours that we have hostile feelings about David except in so far as we have harboured them malevolently. They arrived unannounced and we do not need to blame ourselves. So having acknowledged that we do indeed feel hostile, the other way to handle the situation is to choose to act effectually. There are two strands to what we need to do which can be worked at separately but often merge together since they do in fact belong to one another.

The first strand is to make some kind of investigation into the reasons why we feel hostile, to explore the mystery. The reasons are occasionally obvious or apparently obvious, but deeper issues invariably lie behind that. An outsider can often give us a great deal of help here, probing the reasons with us. Bold friends, attentively listened to, can have some unpalatable as well as some amazingly heart-warming things to say about us if we will give them an opportunity to say them. We might slowly learn some of the reasons why David rather than Jack raises our temperature like that, how that interaction has elements of other relationships in our pasts which have caused us to throw up barriers against him. We start a fascinating quest.

The other strand is actively to raise the matter with David. It is with David that we are having difficulty and it is he therefore, one way or another, who is likely in the end to give us the most information about it. We may not know whether he has similar difficulties with us and we certainly will not know the exact nature of that difficulty though naturally, as I have discussed earlier, we will often project our hostility on to him and ask everybody else why David is so hostile to us. Our integrity demands that we should not keep him in ignorance of what we feel and even though it is paralyzingly difficult at times to act in this way it is amazing how frequently the response is less antagonistic than we feared. Not always of course, but either way we learn a great deal.

The two strands intertwine. The action of talking to David feeds the thinking about the mystery. Pennies start dropping as the relationship moves on. We no longer confront the hostility and attempt to batter it into submission. We explore it, bring it home to rest in us. We understand that it has not been a matter of a foreign hostile feeling taking up residence in us but rather that we have been a hostile person for this and that sort of reason, that we are now less so, that the hostility is less of a mystery than it was and that next time we feel hostile we shall cope with it more easily.

While it is always true, I believe, that a serious attention to the history of an emotion we experience is the royal road to freedom from its ensnarement, emotions do not always lend themselves to exactly this approach. It is quite conceivable, as I forecast in the last chapter, that it will be either inappropriate or impossible to take up the matter with the person concerned.

Suppose a man or woman in their forties, happily married, finds himself or herself sexually aroused by a seventeen-year-old, which is not in the least uncommon or surprising, even among Christians. It would rarely be helpful to raise the matter with the young person concerned. Their experience of loving is underdeveloped and naturally focused on people of their own age. Any talk with them directly about sexual love from a person whom they might think to be well past it could be puzzling, embarrassing and possibly dangerous for both parties. Indeed we could easily convince ourselves that this is an obvious case for direct 'control' of our emotions. It is perfectly obvious, we might say, that people with waning sexual powers may wish to assert their sexual identity and nobody denies that many a seventeen-year-old is exceedingly attractive. This does not require any thinking about. All we need to do is to put all such thoughts firmly behind us and to return swiftly to our spouse.

That may be the proper destination of our adventure but the means of arriving there needs to be well handled. We do not need to look further than the disturbing revelations about the sexual habits of certain American television evangelists to know that we can easily deceive ourselves where sex is concerned. Such evangelists displayed the classic approach to sexual arousal. Finding themselves sexual beings outside as well as inside the boundaries of their marriage and believing that they were wrong to be so, they first of all denied that they were improperly sexual, although they secretly fed their repressed sexuality with pornographic magazines, and then projected their forbidden sex on to others who displayed such 'bad' behaviour, the strength of their bitter denunciations matching their fears of their own natures.

The old familiar habits of denial and projection were at work. They were foolish, frightened men who had not taken stock of their emotional lives, had not seriously thought about it. For what is always at issue in such matters is not the general nature of humanity's sexuality but the particularity of our own. In general, sexuality is much the same wherever we look; in particular, our own sexuality is frightening, exciting, bewildering and extremely hard to sort out satisfactorily. For each of us individually sex is a completely new discovery. We can no more know what our sexuality is like without experiencing it – understanding of course that sexuality is experienced in all manner of ways short of sexual intercourse – than we can feel what a foreign country is like without living in it for a time.

So it is not enough for the older man or woman to turn their backs resolutely upon their feelings for the seventeen-year-old. The feelings need attention, careful attention lest they go underground. But since it is inappropriate to enter upon that voyage of discovery with the young person, substitutes need to be found and the natural substitute in many cases might be their own partner. If a passing attraction is in danger of turning into an obsession there is at least a circumstantial case for believing that there might be something wrong with legitimate sex and attention at that point could be well rewarded. Our sexuality is very deep-rooted in us and very precious. It deserves and repays our care.

There are other times when it is not just inadvisable but impossible to take up an emotional matter directly. When we think about sadness, for instance, it is hard to see how anybody else is involved at all. Sadness is so very much a private and internal emotion and one which few of us, anyway to start with, view pejoratively. Genuine sadness is usually brought about by loss, tangible things like a job we very much wanted or a piece of jewellery of sentimental value, intangible ones like a loss of respect of a purpose in life. Above all we are sad if we lose by departure or death somebody that we deeply love. In each case sadness is characterized by the withdrawal of what we wanted rather than the confrontation of what we do not want, which is the mark of many other emotions like anger, jealousy and fear.

In such simple cases it is a matter of working through the sadness, supported by the love of those who remain, until we come out the other end. Even here in such uncomplicated sadness we do well to reflect upon the process as it proceeds, seeking the active participation of our allies so that we may learn compassion through the process of healing.

At other times it is more complex. We may have had an actual loss which has been the trigger for our emotions or we may simply be sick at heart without any clear understanding of what has brought it about. Depression sets in which in severe cases needs the attention of a specialist. Whether mild or severe, such depression is often caused by the inability to come to terms with other losses which have their roots in our pasts.

I saw over several months, for example, a man whose persistent depression in his thirties arose largely through the loss of his grandfather when he was aged about twelve. His grandfather, who lived in a cottage by the river, was the one person who had given him loving attention. He would escape from a thoughtlessly savage father and an indifferent mother down to the cottage and they would walk hand in hand through the reeds and learn about the natural world, brushing against the wild flowers, interpreting the sounds of the water and the wind. When his grandfather died he had been to the funeral but had not, as he said, been notably moved. He watched the coffin into the earth and went home without a tear.

But with that coffin had been buried the only love he had known and under a fairly bland exterior came to birth a settled distrust of life and those who lived it. Married for some years and the father of three children, he was walking through life in a dream. Exhortations to 'snap out of it' or to 'cheer up' had been totally ineffective for years. He had been forced by his parents to control what he took to be all his bad emotions and the only good emotion he knew was taken away from him when he was twelve. Those who later bade him exercise control were only reinforcing the hurts and the failures of those early years.

When he began to come to terms with all of that, his grandfather had been long dead and he had therefore to find substitutes in the form of a number of able carers through whom he could work himself back into the loving human race again. Through great tribulation and with much courage he did so, reliving the loss of his grandfather head on, and the last I heard of him he was well on the way to becoming an effective enabler of other human beings in similar difficulties.

The main tools then that we possess to take control of our emotions are our dual capacities to reflect upon our own behaviour and to choose to risk meeting other people's worlds. As we ponder upon our histories and tentatively test out our reflections in practice, little by little we shift ground internally and the old battles in which we attempted to take our emotions by the scruff of the neck and force them to our will become irrelevant, for we have already moved on. It is the release of our own direct control in the form I have described it which brings in a new sort of control through the back door.

It is not to be thought, however, that this is any sort of magic process, an infallible formula for integrated living. As I have remarked before, human life cannot be reduced to rules and we all know that there are always further peaks past each plateau. Success here is hard to measure and Christians should not be surprised to find that what we initially took to be a loss turns out to be a gain ('Whoever wants to save his own life will lose it; but whoever loses his life for my sake will find it', Matt. 16.25). We must expect to find ourselves often mystified, scared at approaching people and cold-shouldered by them, sexually compromised, misunderstood and not infrequently overpowered by this or that feeling. A risk is precisely what it says, a step away from what is familiar to us, relieving ourselves of complete control of what happens, putting ourselves at the mercy of other people and events. Such behaviour may produce this result or that but the gospels do not lead us to suppose that we need be unduly anxious if we land up, as we shall at times, with what appear to us to be lamentable failures. Guilt can be a useful pointer to the right path but it is a deplorable companion to accompany us on the way and we need quickly to reassure ourselves of the grace and forgiveness of a Father who gathers up his skirts and runs to meet us in our indiscretions (Luke 15.20).

There may be readers who will be glad to hear me say that. They may have several reservations over the sort of things I have been saying about the control of the emotions. They may not, to be frank, find the suggestions quite religious enough. Like Naaman who objected to Elisha's rather secular approach to the curing of his leprosy (II Kings 5.11, 'Naaman left in a rage, saying, "I thought that he would at least come out to me, pray to the Lord his God, wave his hand over the diseased spot, and cure me"'), they might miss any reference to the activity of the Holy Spirit or to prayer. I have, I confess, rather taken that for granted. If we do not pray our way through the difficulties we have with our feelings and their control we are not in the least likely to take them in hand. In prayer, in which Jesus bids us not to 'use a lot of meaningless words' (Matt. 6.7), we are confronted with the silence of God and our helplessness without his grace ('close the door and pray to your Father who is there in the secret place', Matt. 6.6) but also with the call to match our actions to our prayers ('ask and you will receive, seek and you will find, knock and the door will be opened unto you', Luke 11.9). The doors of other people's lives, where they link with our own, will not open unless we knock and enter.

More than that, I believe the approach suggested bears resemblances in two respects to the ways that Jesus would use with people. He was adamant that he could not heal unless there was faith to respond to. On the other hand the faith invited needed to be only at a simple level. It was enough that they believed he could heal. In his healing ministry he made no demands – or anyway no recorded demands – for religious faith. He almost took for granted that they would follow religious practices ('Go and show yourself to the priest', Luke 5.14) and he otherwise simply demanded that they believed in him (Mark 5.34, 9.23, Luke 5.20, 7.9 etc). He was saying therefore that nothing could happen until they were prepared to take a risk – which is precisely true, I believe, about the healing of relationships.

We may also note that Jesus had a way of forcing people back on their own resources. The main evidence of this is the way that he kept teaching the people by parables which he is never recorded as having explained to anybody except occasionally his disciples. The truth was to be apprehended slant-wise and the people would have to make up their own minds and arrive at their own responses. He continued this practice in small groups and with individuals, directly inviting but never forcing a response.

Asked a question by a lawyer he asked another one back (Luke 10.25, 26). Confronted by a blind man whose needs must have been perfectly obvious, Jesus enquired, 'What do you want me to do for you?' (Mark 10.51) Sitting at meat with Simon the Pharisee who had failed to offer his famous guest even the simplest courtesies, he told a story about a moneylender who had a small and a large debtor and let them both off. Innocently he enquired which would love the moneylender more, thus allowing the embarrassed Simon to condemn himself out of his own mouth (Luke 7.41–3. See also John 5.6, Luke 8.25, Mark 8.14–21 etc.). It was not enough that people should make some sort of inner commitment to God. The faith he required, like that required of us in the matter of the emotions, had to be an active response and it was that active faith which both demonstrated and sealed the inner commitment. 'Follow me' was Jesus' invariable call and the disciples took the risk of laying down their nets there and then and walking off at his side.

Others may have misgivings about this approach to the control of the emotions on more practical grounds. 'Heavens!' they might say, 'life is busy enough as it is without going through all that kind of process with everybody I meet. I simply have neither the time nor the energy to sift through all my emotions like that. Anyway I'm a practical sort of person and I'm not very good at all this introspection. It seems to me a rather self-centred exercise and we should all be better employed out helping our neighbours.'

I have some sympathy with such a response. My approach does on the face of it seem to imply a lifelong imprisonment to self-analysis and a sort of utilitarian approach to human relationships which leaves love a long way behind. Perhaps I may begin to counter such objections in terms of the way we might run an office or a busy home. Most of us understand that it is quite possible to be obsessive about such activities. Some people make endless lists, keep things precisely in the same position, answer letters immediately, renew the carpets every five and a half years, keep strict files. They say they are 'keeping on top of it all', but we cannot help feeling that most of the time the organization is keeping on top of them. I would not wish anybody to become similarly obsessive about their relationships.

Yet we know that a reasonable order in an office or home is part of its successful management. Such order is not an extraneous imposition but an integral part of it. It enables, leaves time for, everything else to happen because we are not continually trying to find our way about.

It is in some such way that I understand us launching into a venture like this. Our emotions are never going to go away and we may as well therefore bring them into some sort of order lest we should be entirely at their mercy. We have to begin the process with one person or in one eventuality of our lives and it will unquestionably at first take up some time, as it takes time to organize office or home. We cannot in a fortnight review lives which have been decades in the building nor can we expect to reach a secure relationship with anybody in a couple of meetings. But what we can be assured of is this: that, in the same way that an office or a home run more freely when the basic organization is sorted out, so our emotions, once we take them in hand, will fall more easily into place. We do not have to do the same work twice. Once we have tackled David about our hostility, or have come to understand the basis of our current irrational fear, we never again have to do the same work from scratch. We have moved on. The next time we meet a hostile person, the next time we wake frightened in the night, our mind and our heart will have joined forces to make more sense of what is happening to us, and the new enemy is easier to meet or we fall quietly to sleep again.

We are therefore now freed to be human and all our relationships begin to make more sense. It is an enormously fascinating exercise and we have to be careful not to allow the means to govern the end, becoming unhealthily introspective, as the organization of the home or office can become obsessional. The way to counter that is to remember that the task is a two-fold one, partly implying some self-analysis but also requiring the testing of that analysis with people, who will rarely allow us to get away with much. Nor need we feel that the exercise is only for a certain sort of inward-looking person and that it will be too hard for us. We all of us have inner lives which urgently require expression and it is my experience, as I have said, that the elucidation of that inner life comes at the interface between us and another person, and in most cases the opening up of that interface requires only courage.

Experience shows that there are some means of bringing this desirable state of affairs about which are more useful than others, and I will end this chapter by mentioning one or two of these clues. Not only have I found them personally helpful but they are in themselves part of the pilgrimage.

Let us look for instance at how we hear one another. We were brought up in the perfectly sound belief that the way to get answers is to ask questions. We asked questions of our parents and teachers and expected them to know the answers or at least to find out. We brought into adulthood, therefore, a pattern of asking questions as the means of finding answers, and in many of our adult affairs the equation still stands. I have not tired of telling that the establishment of the fact, as distinguished from the feelings, is indispensable for the right ordering of our emotions, and facts are often elicited by questions. But not always, and especially not as we attempt to establish relationships. How often have we experienced this sort of thing? A wife is talking to her husband. 'What's the matter, darling?' 'Nothing.' 'It doesn't look like nothing. Is it work?' 'No.' 'Is it the children then? Have they been bothering you?' 'No, it's nothing I tell you.' 'A funny sort of nothing then to make you look so black.' 'Look, I've told you. It's nothing. Just get off my back, will you?' 'Oh, I know. It's me again, I suppose. Isn't that it? What have I done this time? Uh?' At which point husband storms out of the room!

The wife is concerned because her husband is manifestly upset, and he recognizes her concern even though she may be part of the problem. Yet her series of questions, well-meant as they are, make it increasingly probable that he will be unable to reveal what is troubling him. He feels them as intrusive, as an invasion of his privacy, even as a means of her establishing her ascendancy by making him submissive to her interrogation. Although her questions arise out of a genuine love for him, all they have succeeded in doing is making him more furious and cut off than ever, while she is left feeling hard done by.

There is another way which will make her more vulnerable. It is to state what she feels rather than to try to elicit what the other feels. The wife might say, 'Darling, when you look like that I feel like a child again.' Husband looks at her. 'My dad used to make me feel like that when I came in too late.' 'I'm not your dad.' 'No.' There may not be any more said but they leave one another more fruitfully than before. A lot has been revealed in a very short exchange. She is talking about what men have been, and are, to her and about the clear distinction, as well as the overlapping, between father and husband. Her feelings are now at stake as well as his. He has been forced to no revelation, only encouraged to them by the fact that she has made herself more open. And it all comes about not by demanding that he should reveal what he feels but by her stating what she feels.

It is easy to become confused here. It is undeniably very hard to distinguish our own feelings from those that belong to others. Because our feelings are so much part of us, what we live with every day, we cannot believe that somebody else might feel differently, or rather we can believe it with our minds but not in our heart of hearts. So we impute what we feel to others as if it belongs to them as well. 'I'm sure you feel ...' we say to each other, though there is absolutely no way that we can be sure of any such thing. Nobody knows how anybody else feels until they say so, and our aim needs to be to allow other people the space to say what they feel and to believe them when they reveal that their feelings are unlike our own.

It takes much practice to view our feelings with that sort of inner dispassionate eye we all possess. Time and again our feelings burble out of us unthinkingly and it takes real and unremitting effort to be honest to what we feel. When our feelings arrive all in a jumble and we tend to leap into the old familiar ways of exchange with those around us it takes genuine effort to pause and to think to ourselves, 'Now what do I really feel at the moment?' Often we give up, saying, 'I don't know.' Sometimes that really means, 'I daren't say.'

8

Emotion in the Church

We have travelled a long way since we heard the stories of Alphonse and Torrey in the first chapter, and though we may be a little clearer about how an individual Christian may order his emotional life it is still not apparent exactly how this relates to emotional religion or whether it is right that such insights should be fed into the life of the church and if so in what form. One part of us rebels against the boredom that much church worship inspires while another either craves, or is repelled by, what we call the 'emotionalism' that seems the only alternative. Either nothing happens in church and we wonder why we bother, or too much happens and we retreat, embarrassed, into our shell.

The minister may often exhort us to 'take our faith out into the world and live it'. It may be we sometimes feel that he has it the wrong way round and that it would be a more helpful first step to bring some of the ordinary world into our faith so that we could make some connections. This chapter is an attempt to see if that might be the way forward.

Initially nothing can relieve us of the responsibility of taking steps to come to terms with our own emotions, using perhaps some of the suggestions already made in this book. The central part of this task, the foundation of all human and Christian living, is to learn how to love.

It is hard to think of any emotion which does not in the end bear some kind of close relation to love. Anger, as I have described it, is the spur to the restoration of our brotherhood and sisterhood before God. To feel cruel is a distortion of love, a bitter response to relationships that never satisfied us. Shyness is the fear of love, the belief that we are not worthy of it or will be rejected from it. Kindness, sexiness, affection and joy are the expressions of love, arising out of the serene knowledge that we are and have been loved. Sadness is the loss of love. Jealousy arises at the point when we are having to reconcile one love with another and to discover how we may love, and be loved by, more than one person at a time.

Loving is such fun! It is a shame if we deny ourselves the opportunity of exploring it with lots of different people. And once we start, it almost seems too good to be true that this is the way God intends, and has always intended, that we should become his children. Naturally at the same time we lay ourselves open to being hurt, as the forms of love just described make quite plain. But being hurt is not the antithesis of loving, it is part of its nature. To refuse to allow ourselves to be hurt makes it certain that we shall not love.

We need to return time and again to Jesus' loving. All ages, sexes and races came to him and he received them all un-hurriedly, expecting and in some cases (Mark 10.14) demanding a closeness, turning none away though retreating from them all when he felt the need, and at the same time refusing to compromise either his or their integrity. We all know how quickly such behaviour met with a bleak response among those who should have known better and I have described earlier my belief that the church was unable to take quite to its heart so radical a message. Even so there is plenty of evidence in the New Testament (Luke 6.27–36, John 13.1–17, 15.11–17, Rom. 13.8–10. I John 4.7–21 etc) that the first Christians tried earnestly to put his message into practice, and themselves swiftly paid the price for it.

So that is the task of the individual Christian and any of us can start anywhere with that. We need only one other person with whom to set about the adventure, and most of us begin with a member of our own family. Once we have achieved some confidence here (as of course many of us have done long ago) we shall wish to make all our relationships as profitable and we might dare to intrude emotion into the life of the church. The strange thing is that emotions are so immediately recognizable by human beings that even one person on one occasion can bring about a shift in a local church, can compel it to introduce into itself the reality of what people feel, rather than what they think, or fantasize about, or just ordinarily do.

Every church has meetings and most of us attend some of them. Their achievements are not always glorious. They often proceed at two levels. At one level the leader or chairperson attempts to bring about a planned end or to discover a goal and the members, more or less reluctantly, assist him or her. At another level the members' real feelings are expressed through darting looks, a shifting in their seats, quiet mutterings to their neighbours or a stare out of the window. When the meeting draws to a close those latent feelings will immediately be expressed privately as members seek out a known ally and rumble on about what they really feel about the subject and course of the meeting. An end has been achieved but at the expense of the members' inner feelings about that end.

There will usually be at least one person in any meeting who appears to be open and honest. He or she will intervene with a loud, 'Well, I'll tell you what I think about it.' Everybody sighs quietly. They know well enough what he or she thinks about it for they have often heard it all before and they know that the member takes pride in 'saying what I think'. The approach is a good deal less helpful than first appears. It has the virtue of honesty but it also tends to want its own way and to be sullen or dismissive if it does not get it. There is something of the bully, the attacker, in the approach and other members fall swiftly, though usually silently, into a defensive position.

There is another way. The local churches have gathered for an interdenominational meeting during the Week of Prayer for Christian Unity. A dozen or so are studying the Bible and making friendly noises to one another, for we all need to encourage one another in love. One participant is a Baptist who, nobody else knows, used to be a member of the Church of England. She sits quietly for some time as the other members smile and seek for helpful messages from the text. During a pause she says, 'I wish I felt it was as easy as that. I was once a member of the Church of England and I felt it rejected me rather than the other way round. I feel bitter about that now. I don't know how to achieve unity with those who turned their backs on me.'

Immediately the group has hit reality because they have heard what she felt rather than what she thought. It is clear, as it is always clear to us when it happens, that the words have come out of her heart and that they are strictly relevant to the subject of Christian unity. Feelings have taken root in the meeting and permission is thereby granted for other people to share their feelings too.

Many groups are ill-disposed to have their feelings exposed in such a way and a familiar method of making sure that the revelations do no further harm is to turn the speaker into a client. To reveal feelings like that shows that she has a 'problem', and problems are things everybody understands. So the whole group can turn its attention on her and attempt to find solutions to it, thereby at once setting aside the deep-seated challenge to themselves that lies at the root of the words. To say 'Poor thing!' covers, apparently in a Christian way, their refusal to examine any rejections they too may have suffered.

So the lady, if she is wise and can resist the temptation to be the focus of their collective care, will gently refuse their instant attention, return the feelings back into the centre of the meeting. 'How do you feel about it?' The group is now forced to come to terms with this quiet dissenter and there will often be one brave soul who will follow her lead, resulting perhaps in a discussion which talks less about theology than about the feelings that keep Christians apart. Few people will leave that meeting 'unmoved', as we say, that is whose emotions have not been personally engaged. Reactions may as well be those of hurt and anger as of concern and love, but nobody is in any doubt that they are real.

After the meeting, of course, it may well be required of Christian love that a member of the group, preferably one from the church which rejected her, takes up with the lady personally the hurts she has suffered.

Another means of introducing emotional reality into the life of the church community is so homespun that I am somewhat diffident about mentioning it. It stems from that cheering message in St Luke's version of the Sermon on the Mount. 'Give and it shall be given to you. Good measure, pressed down, shaken together and running over will be poured into your lap' (Luke 6.38). The generosity of God is absolutely overwhelming and to lay claim to that openness of heart we need do no more than to be generous ourselves. It is possible, without undue distortion, to encapsulate the entire gospel in that one word 'generosity'.

Now the natural response to generosity is gratitude which is why, though not nearly frequently enough, we are urged to make thanksgiving one of the major parts of our prayers. You would expect therefore that Christians would be the very first people to express their thanks to each other. Yet alas! I have never noticed that we are any better at it than anybody else. To give people thanks is a recognition of their value to us. It is a way of making those real, personal contacts we run away from. The more carefully we look the more we see how much we all receive from each other, and in the exchange of gratitude for those gifts one heart speaks to another.

There is more than that. We need also to say openly what we value in each other. Quite early on in a confirmation course I used to make it a practice to offer a blank piece of paper and a pencil to each candidate. We all went away into a corner of the room and wrote down about each other, 'What I like about Jane/Tom is ...' After ten minutes I collected in the papers and on a large sheet of paper on the wall wrote against each of our names the positive things each of us had written. The result was marvellously affirming. I was myself always moved by what they had written, not least astonished at the acute observations of this succession of youngsters. Few of them had ever seen listed a record of some of their positive attributes. Peers are too shy to do so and parents more frequently list their shortcomings. Because all our emotions had become engaged the exercise always shifted the group on to a new level of understanding.

Why do we find it so hard to say the nice things to each other? It is not because we do not recognize other people's values. We will talk for hours to other people about our friends and how good they are in this, that or the other respect. We can sometimes bring ourselves to expostulate to our friends or fellow church members about their failings and drawbacks; to speak to them directly about their value is usually too hard. It is my experience that we can bear hearing about our imperfections provided only that we have first heard what the speaker values in us. To be prepared to practise this exchange within the church is one further road to making real connections between our faith and our reality as human beings.

I came upon another route almost be accident, though once achieved it was strange that I had never quite seen it before. I have written more fully about the occasion elsewhere.[1] I had noted in the Church of England's endless debates over twenty to thirty years about the remarriage of divorced people in church that apart from the statutory composition of the various synods the debate was conducted very largely between ministers. The House of Bishops of that church, for example made a definitive statement in 1985 which reads:

> There is a substantial number of those in the Church who believe in good conscience that a 'second' marriage is possible in some cases. Those clergy who take this considered view are free under the provision of civil law, to allow such 'second' marriages. The ultimate decision in such cases must be a matter for the clergyman concerned.

It suddenly struck me that it could not possibly be right that ministers should have such a prominent authority in a debate that very closely concerned about one-third of the adult British population, and I decided – and this was the only decision that I made in the whole debate – that I would throw open the question to the consideration of the church I served. Having talked it over with two sensitive churchwardens I produced a paper for the church council which I modestly took to be factual and balanced, showing the arguments on both sides. I ended the paper with three examples of situations in which I thought they might like to consider a measure of discrimination. I wondered, for instance, whether they might like to treat differently couples who were or were not members of the church or others who were marrying for a third time.

I was utterly unprepared for the laity's reaction to this paper. A whole cauldron of emotions, which must have been simmering for years, suddenly boiled over. Some people attacked me furiously for what they took to be unChristian discrimination. Others were in tears, deeply hurt at what they saw as an assault upon their integrity. Others again were shocked that the church's traditional teaching should be brought so blatantly out into the open for discussion and some expressed bewildered incomprehension over the whole matter. Second marriages appeared unexpectedly from behind long-established unions and church members revealed themselves in a new light.

I was told very firmly that I should revise my paper which in its new form in due course was circulated among all the church members and culminated in an open meeting in church one November evening. It was one of the most moving meetings I have ever attended. People hesitantly at first and then with growing confidence as they listened to other stories told us about the hurts, failures and triumphs of their marriages and of the convictions that they now held because of their experiences. They were not predictable. Divorced and remarried couples present told us how contented they had been and still were with the Service of Blessing they had been offered, and stalwart citizens in high office, married to one person all their lives, startled us with their conviction that remarriage in church should be permitted.

The debate wended its way, at a rather less intensely emotional level, for some eighteen months until the church decided by a substantial majority to permit the remarriage of divorced people in church under certain conditions which we need not go into here. For the purpose of telling that story is to demonstrate that, once they are permitted to do so, members of the church are well capable not only of displaying a high level of emotion over matters close to their hearts, which we might expect, but also of harnessing that energy to give a serious, theological attention to an acutely demanding subject. Furthermore, out of that debate grew a concern for the inadequacy with which the local church was preparing all couples for marriage, and a direct consequence was the eventual training of a dozen church members who committed themselves to planning and staffing regular mandatory marriage preparation groups for all those being married in the parish church.

The moral of the story must be that it is often we ministers who are most responsible for keeping the cork in the bottle of the church's emotions and therefore for keeping reality at the church door.

For me the remarriage debate was initially a thoroughly alarming experience and my first instinct was rapidly to cork up the bottle again before anybody got hurt. Maturer reflection led me to see how manipulative such an action would be and how fearful I was of allowing the hurt to surface. I had responsibility for maintaining the unity of the local church but not at the expense of the members' integrity. It was inevitable that people's feelings on such a matter would differ, and differ profoundly, but it was no business of mine to maintain the fiction that it was otherwise. Moreover my better understanding of the faith knew that love only grows through exposure, and in the end my only task was to ensure that everybody was careful to listen to everybody else and did not indulge in emotional bulldozing.

It is easy to see that there are other volatile subjects – the authority of the minister, for instance, homosexuality, loving and abusing children, even the use of anger – which, if set free in the church, could be similarly liberating, could ensure that the church addresses itself to the emotional reality of people's lives. Nevertheless one warning is necessary. It is quite essential that all such issues should be addressed with a complete integrity, out of a deep concern for the matter in question and with a determination that we shall risk ourselves to the grace of God. It is not permissible that any of us should juggle with each others' emotions to obtain an end, however desirable. Such behaviour will be instantly detected and resented.

One of the main functions of a church is to worship God, and we need to consider how far we should permit, encourage or deplore emotion in worship. Opinions differ sharply at this point, indeed each of us may have an ambivalent attitude ourselves, so we need to walk warily. There are not many, however, who would deny that there are some services at which emotions are quite appropriate.

People are expected to weep at funerals and though a few may be critical because the mourners cannot 'pull themselves to-gether' most of us at least tolerate some tears. Weddings and baptisms are occasions of rejoicing and we do not disapprove too much of the high spirits and cheerful banter, the chuckings under the chin and the admiring grins. People are moved at the Christmas Midnight Mass by candlelight and like to come and bellow the harvest hymns. At Easter they love the church full of daffodils and the joyous liturgy, full of the hopes that spring brings, giving them the prospect that their lives are ultimately worthwhile. All such emotion is acceptable. Yet it is episodic, something of an intrusion into the even tenor of everyday worship. Is it more than a coincidence that they are also the occasions when the church is most full?

I believe it is. People come to these services because they lend some sort of sense to their lives, because they can make connections between their inner experiences and the offering of the church, because the worship fits. Their emotions are engaged – their sadness and fears, their happiness and joy, their love and hopes and sense of togetherness. The fact that, without it must be said undue encouragement, they pour into these services is evidence that they find meaning there, and the church has not yet learned to distinguish clearly enough between the task of exploring these values with them in the light of the Christian conviction and peremptorily attempting to gain more adherents.

'Baptism statistics', it is said, 'have suggested that the Church of England has accepted pastoral and catechetical responsibility for over one-third of the child population, or some 2,881,000 infants, children and young people under the age of fourteen.'[2] Several million adults in the British Isles therefore, from motives which are self-generated (for I have never heard of churches going out to search for infant baptism candidates), seek some kind of recognition of their children by God through the church. That they feel it is very important is revealed by their intense anger if for any reason baptism is refused.

Most ministers will give some attention to the preparation of these parents and some churches take a wider responsibility, laying on preparation evenings. The focus of that preparation is usually an explanation of the church's understanding of the sacrament of baptism and an encouragement for the whole family, but especially the child, to join the church's membership. There is nothing wrong with that except that it fails to address the inner hopes and yearnings which have brought them there in the first place. Robin Green, in a recent constructive book about worship and liturgy from the perspective of pastoral care, has suggested a fascinating outline for baptism preparation which is strictly relevant to how people live and feel. He suggests a programme like this:

1. An explanation of the significance of the water: what meaning does it have? What do people associate with it? Perhaps people could be encouraged to go on a fantasy journey ...

2. 'Everything is alright'? When a child screams in the middle of the night and a parent gives this assurance are they lying or telling the truth? Where do we get our values from? Who am I? What do we want our children to be? ...

3. Do parents experience violence in themselves? Or towards their children? What do they feel about violence towards children? ...

4. What does 'home' mean? Do words like 'belonging' and 'together' have important meanings? What are they? What does 'finding a home' imply? ...

5. What kind of community do I want to belong to? What kind of world do we want for our children? ...

6. What would you be prepared to sacrifice for your child? What do you really believe in? What do you have faith in? Would you be prepared to die for anything? ...[3]

It is too much to expect that any unchurched parent could cope with all of that, but any of those questions would lead them all directly into their feelings about the nature of love and hate, their fears for their child and themselves, the way people live together. They would not be struggling to make sense of unfamiliar theological or ecclesiastical ideas but would be hearing the church address their needs and emotions at exactly the point they have requested it. Nor would the question be irrelevant to the church's missionary task. We could scarcely argue that an exploration into values, the source of values, and the meaning of belonging, community and sacrifice are not central to the Christian message. When the church offers a loving attention to people's real needs it is doing no more than mirror the way God deals with us.

A quick glance down the 'Thanks' advertisement column of any local newspaper will demonstrate how appreciative people are of the church's care at a time of bereavement. The church's traditional role is to bind up the wounds of the broken-hearted and many churches and ministers do it well particularly at the point immediately after death. To deal with this kind of emotion raises no hackles in the church perhaps because it offers no challenge to the church's authority. Tears flow and are gently wiped away.

Yet somehow the message that it is permissible to shed tears and allow space to our sadder emotions remains latent and hidden and certainly does not escape much out of the confines of the mourning process. Even there the recently bereaved may soon become quite desperately hurt by their isolation. They have to bear both the loss and the embarrassment of those who cannot sustain their attention to grief. Widows and widowers tell of friends who look away, or even cross the street, when they see them in public until they can be sure that the bereaved have, as they say, 'got over it'. To maintain signs of grief after a rather short acceptable period often produces irritation rather than sympathy and a suspicion that the bereaved are indulging themselves.

A recent television programme told of a young Australian woman, Suzi, who, with impressive courage, was facing death from Aids, achingly cared for by her husband who was giving her magnificent support through her illness. Their two-year-old son, equally cherished, was another carrier of the virus. As, a week or two before her death, Suzi and her husband lay side by side on her bed, gently caressing each other, they talked about what it would be like after she had died. He did not display much emotion. He said, 'I shall be all right on the outside but I don't know how I shall cope on the inside. I don't know.' And as tears poured down her cheeks he wiped them away with his fingers and kept saying, 'Don't cry, don't cry, don't cry.' She made a fine effort to restrain her tears but there was no doubt that the quiet mingling of their tears would have brought a greater healing and I kept wondering what it was that prevented his outside, in these extreme conditions, matching his inside.

Churches need to be places where we can bear one another's tears. As Suzi's husband saw his tears perhaps as a denial of his manhood, so many Christians see them as a denial of their faith. To cry at the death of a loved one is a sign of a lack of belief in God's care, a selfish flaunting of one's own feelings, a defiance of trust. The courage of Christians who bear their losses with a consistent cheerfulness is impressive, misplaced and dangerous. Few can fail to be amazed at such a triumph of belief over natural feeling but it arises out of a seriously defective theology in which God is seen to be the conqueror rather than the saviour of the world. Such a belief leads to either a dangerous triumphalism or, when that ultimately fails, a deep-seated despair both of which destroy our trust in the grace of God. Tears are not a sign of faithlessness; they are rather a wondrous gift of God, designed to reveal and to heal our helplessness.

Grace Jantzen tells the story of an early bishop Nonnus who was leading a group of fellow bishops in an outdoor Bible study

when a prostitute, Pelagia, and her entourage paraded by
'resplendent in jewellery and very little else'. She continues:

> The other bishops hide their faces in the scapulars; but
> Nonnus, after gazing after her with rapt attention, asks them
> why they did not rather rejoice in her beauty. When they did
> not reply he buried his face on his knees over the holy Bible
> which he held in his hands and all his emotions came out in
> tears ...

When he returned to his lodgings he 'threw himself on the
ground with his face to the floor ... and wept for many hours'
and his deacon commented, 'that day was a great festival of tears
for us'.[4] 'A great festival of tears'. What an unexpected sort of
picture for today's church! Not a self-indulgent attempt to gain
other people's sympathy but a natural response to creation's
magnificence and to the world's hard-heartedness, notably, as
we observe in the account, the world in the shape of prudish
bishops, and an enthusiastic embracing of the means God has
given us of uniting ourselves emotionally with his realities.
It is always a great day for the church's mission when in the
name of Christ his people have their arms around one another
and tears roll down their cheeks. 'Weep with those who weep'
(Rom. 12.15).

But, the reader may enquire, you would not want the church to
have festivals of anger, despair, jealousy or fear as well, would you?
These are also emotional realities, and in your view realities which
have no inherent moral content. Surely such emotions cannot
properly have a place in the life and worship of the church?

The fact is, however, that one way or another these emotions
are always present in the life of the church and its worship
anyway, but usually unconstructively. Members of the church
are angry with the minister or with the group of elders but do
not tell them so. Perhaps in the past having too frequently
received a brush-off from those in authority, they talk acidly to
sympathetic fellow-members or listen with tight lips and closed
ears to the minister as he fulminates in the pulpit about the lack
of forgiveness in the church and tries to avoid eyeing the
suspected offenders malevolently. Anger in practice is given a
wide permission of expression except where there might be
some chance of healing the break-down in relationships that its
presence testifies to.

As I have often observed already, jealousy is a sign of our struggle to love more than one person at a time. Jealousy will therefore be widely present in the church as in any other mixed organization together with all the additional troubles that attend upon our worshipping a jealous God. We shall resent the attention given to members of the church who make heavy demands on everybody's time, we shall yearn for a more personal care to be given to our aches and bruises, and we shall have to find ways of reconciling the exclusive demands of God with the claims of those who can rightly expect our attention. These are not sinful, guilt-invoking conditions which must be crushed under the heavy boot of righteousness. They are simply the evidence of our human lot and become sinful only when we do not take pains to solve the dilemmas and allow competitiveness or possessiveness their head.

Fear and despair can lead to an utterly frozen church. Fear may expose, for instance, an autocratic minister, a childish faith, or a real hazard to the community such as the widespread ecclesiastical obsession with financial security. Despair in a church refuses to believe that the gospel can be genuinely heard or be really effective in today's world, feels that certain personal or national problems are inherently insoluble, look at fellow-Christians with lustreless eyes never expecting to find anything new in any of them.

Nobody denies that churches can do without such feelings. But where they exist they need to be addressed. There is no point in wringing our hands and calling down the wrath of God. Fears and despair have well-founded roots in the experience of ourselves and our communities. It is right to be afraid of autocracy. People find it difficult to hear good news in a world that is preoccupied with defending itself against real or imagined enemies. We do not need to crush our fears and despair with a cold dismissiveness or angry denunciations, playing the familiar game of replacing an unpalatable feeling with a more acceptable one. We need gently to draw all such feelings out into the open, to acknowledge that our world is often hard and unyielding, and to speak to the condition of the community and of the individual as they actually exist.

So we would not wish, naturally, to celebrate negative feelings in the same way as we might choose to have, for example, a Festival of Love (though how many churches have had one of

those?). Yet it would be entirely appropriate to spend a week of a
church's life considering the blacker feelings that come our way,
learning that in those feelings we are neither different from our
fellow-Christians nor abandoned by God. Entitled perhaps a
Festival of Darkness and Light, reality could come tumbling
through the church door as guilt flew out through the east
window.

I cannot finish this brief review of some of the ways in which
churches may discover themselves through their emotions without referring to God's seductive gift of music. It is that part of an
act of worship which belongs to the people. They shout or, more
often, whimper their way through the hymns knowing that
nobody can take this act of participation away from them except
the minister or organist who consistently chooses outlandish
tunes. Hymns are stocked with memories. They are part of our
own personal histories. Resentment is often caused by choirs or
soloists or instrumental groups who hijack the worship, contri-
buting endless items in which the congregation do not have a
part while the latter sit and fidget. It is sad how frequently music
becomes less an expression of our feelings about our life in
Christ than the haunt of acrimony.

Once we are convinced that there is nothing improper in
sitting in church with tears pouring down our cheeks, with grins
splitting our faces, with rapture taking us into seventh heaven or
with a lively urge to get up out of our seat to clap or dance, all
because the music reminds us of emotion-laden people or events
or speaks to levels of our existence which are rarely reached in
other ways, at that moment we are ready to give music its
rightful place in worship. And to reach that point we must be
prepared to give more care, or perhaps a different sort of care,
to church music.

The care I am talking of is the setting loose of our musical
imaginations to see how all kinds of music may lead us into
the way of Christ. Recorded music from Bach to U2; taking
immense trouble to match music, especially hymns, to mood; the
use of 'voice over' during prayers; seeking out local ensembles
and soloists; singing unaccompanied. The creative poverty of
much Sunday by Sunday church music takes some beating.

The church is most dreadfully impoverished because of the
widespread suppression of natural feeling, the silent ruling that
feelings, expressed musically or in any other way, are best kept

under strict control lest they get out of hand. When a church is dull it usually means that it is not engaged with its faith, and that as frequently indicates that it has buried its emotional life. Yet any suggestion that we should give permission to our emotions in our churches at once raises the horrid spectres of a slightly dotty emotionalism which presents itself as the only aternative to dreariness. So we must end by returning to the theme we raised in the first chapter. What is a mature Christian understanding to make of the experience of an Alphonse or a Torrey?

We must first be prepared to welcome with open arms those moments when emotions overwhelm us, both in religion and in other matters of the heart.

When we fall desperately in love, when our whole bodies tremble with relief when a lover comes safely through a car accident, when we laugh and shout for joy because we have suddenly discovered that Jesus lives in us, when tears pour down our cheeks because we have failed again, when our stomachs tighten as we are confronted by a person who has a grievous cause for anger against us and is telling us so, when we are torn in two by conflicting loves and loyalties, when we get the giggles at inappropriate moments and our shoulders heave, when we have a sudden recognition that we hate somebody – all such moments we must cherish. They are times of revelation when we can no longer deceive ourselves. We make contact, unmediated, with our inner realities. We cannot always applaud such moments for reality is not always a pretty sight, nor must we assume that we have caught sight of all there is to see. They are none the less solid ground upon which we can start to rebuild.

We do not need to separate off the specifically religious experiences as if they were of a different nature. Their nature is not different, only their content (you will recall General Skobeleff in the first chapter). When Alphonse felt 'in the bottom of my soul an explosion of the most ardent joy' it was the natural response of his whole created being to an experience of God. It is not offensive to God to say that Alphonse could have used exactly the same words if he had fallen deeply in love with a beautiful girl, it is rather to testify to the unity of our natures and to defend such emotions against the cynics who sabotage them all.

None of our emotions is to be feared, denied, projected, mocked, ignored or rubbished. It is no matter whether they are the passionate experiences that occur in most of our lives only infrequently or the everyday emotions that we have long been used to. Wherever they occur or whatever their degreee of intensity they are to be welcomed as a highway to our God. What we take to be the 'bad' emotions, like hatred or anger or the urge to destroy, are to be cherished as much as the apparently 'good' ones, like excitement or love. Once they have arrived we are responsible for handling them in quite different ways but all of them disclose us as we are rather than as we hope we might be, and to accept them as they come makes it that much less likely that we shall base our lives upon fantasy.

Mind you, while we have to be as innocent as doves in treasuring the emotions that come our way, we have also to be as cunning as serpents in not permitting others to manipulate them. In some churches there is a strong expectation of emotional conformity, governed by the ethos of the community as a whole and often led by the minister who can hold the key which locks up or frees the emotions and dictates which are and which are not permissible.

Those, for instance, who have had the experience of 'speaking in tongues' or those who have 'come to Jesus' in a manner which is silently dictated by the community's collective adventures become an in-group towards whose experiences all are expected to strive. If a member is unable to bring about such an event in his or her life he or she may still be loved after a fashion but is also faintly disapproved or pitied, and urged to greater efforts. There is no more certain way of disguising our emotional realities. Propelled towards a particular communal experience, the member is denied the leisure to recognize his or her own experiences, is often indeed judged harshly for possessing emotions that do not fall within the community's guidelines. Such churches may attract and produce a number of quite scarred human beings. Speaking in tongues and coming to Jesus can manifestly be glorious experiences but they do not define a Christian community any more than falling in love defines a marriage. Emotions are either gifts or they are false.

A single church's, let alone a single minister's, experience is not a reliable guide. Each church's experience needs to be measured against that of the wider church and to be subjected to the scrutiny of Christians who are not members of it. How far such Christian communities do in practice permit this wider scrutiny can often be judged by the way that they deal with intrusive elements. A friend of mine visited a church which had the reputation of being a splendidly loving body, deeply committed to the gospel. They cared for one another and practised a lively worship in which emotions had full play. A man of the highest integrity and one not accustomed to playing games with other people's lives, he came away saying sadly, 'They may have loved one another but they didn't love me.' His emotional reactions fell outside what was acceptable and he was therefore at once excluded.

True emotions, like vagrant Christians, are by nature trespassers. They barge in upon the holiest ground and dare us to make them welcome. Whether we are able to do so is a measure of our Christian maturity and integrity.

Notes

1   The Chaos of our Emotions

[1] Russell Hoban, *The Little Brute Family*, Pan Books 1973.

[2] Charlotte Bronte, *Jane Eyre*, 1847, ch. 2.

[3] William James, *Varieties of Religious Experience*, Riverside Press. Cambridge, Mass. 1902, pp. 224–6.

[4] R. A. Torrey, *Person and Work of the Holy Spirit*, Zondervan, Grand Rapids 1968 p. 244, quoted in Steven Durasoff, *Bright Wind of the Spirit – Pentecostalism Today*, Hodder & Stoughton 1972.

[5] William James, op. cit. pp. 265–6.

[6] Hensley Henson, *Retrospect of an Unimportant Life*, Vol. I, OUP 1943, p. 329.

[7] Hensley Henson, op. cit., Vol. II, pp. 282–3.

[8] Hensley Henson, op. cit. Vol. I, p. 166.

2   Bible and Church

[1] J. Weiss, *Das Urchristentum*, quoted in the Right Revd K. E. Kirk, *The Vision of God*, Longmans 1931, p. 77.

[2] Kirk, op. cit., p. 229.

[3] Gerd Theissen, *Biblical Faith: An Evolutionary Approach*, SCM Press 1984, has a highly original approach to these sorts of issues.

4   Loving

[1] See my *How to be a Christian in Trying Circumstances*, Epworth Press 1985, pp. 97–100

5   Being Angry

[1] Robin Skynner, *One Flesh; Separate Persons*, Constable 1976, p. 44.

[2] Stevie Smith 'The Raven', *The Collected Poems*, Allen Lane, The Penguin Press and New Directions, New York 1975, p. 320. Alistair Campbell in his *Gospel of Anger*, SPCK 1986, p. 66, also makes use of this poem in an excellent book which treats anger more fully.

6 *The Feeling and the Fact*

[1] Charlotte Bronte, *Jane Eyre*, 1847, ch. 2.

[2] *Jane Eyre*, ch. 4.

[3] I am indebted for this image, and for much help in the compilation of this chapter, to James Hillman, *Emotion*, Routledge & Kegan Paul, second revd edn 1962.

8 *Emotion in the Church*

[1] *Crucible*, the quarterly journal of the Church of England's Board for Social Responsibility, January-March 1988, pp.11–13.

[2] *Children in the Way*, Report from the Church of England General Synod's Board of Education, 1988, p. 88.

[3] Robin Green, *Only Connect*, Darton, Longman & Todd 1987, pp. 61–2.

[4] Grace Jantzen in *Theology*, March 1988, referring to Benedicta Ward, *Harlots of the Desert*, Mowbray 1987.